'This has very quickly become my non-fiction pick of the year . . . It's incredible. Feltham's writing is so precise and gentle. She approaches every subject with compassion and a desire to understand.' —Ash Davida Jane, Nine to Noon

'Feltham's voice—smart, hilarious, curious and disarmingly wise—is one I'd read on any topic. I inhaled this collection and urge you to seek out a copy. It will certainly be a standout of the year.' —Maddie Ballard, *The Spinoff*

'*Bad Archive* digs deep into the archives of Feltham's life in a courageous attempt to find meaning and understanding. She skilfully braids together disparate themes of marriage, mothers, fathers, mental illness, drug and alcohol addiction, grief and loss, weaving, archiving and the mutability of memory, all with a compassionate and insightful eye.' —Sue Reidy, *NZ Listener*

'*Bad Archive* dissolves its colours subtly, weaves threads into an archival artwork that only fully reveals its impact once the book is finished and the reader takes a step back to take in its whole—creases, fingerprints, pressed flowers and all.' —Sara Bucher, *Aotearoa New Zealand Review of Books*

Bad Archive

Flora Feltham

TE HERENGA WAKA
UNIVERSITY PRESS

Te Herenga Waka University Press
Victoria University of Wellington
PO Box 600, Wellington
New Zealand
teherengawakapress.co.nz

ISBN 9781776922062

A catalogue record is available from the
National Library of New Zealand

Published with the assistance of a grant from

Printed by Blue Star Wellington

For my family

Contents

On Archiving

The good Archivist is perhaps the most selfless devotee of Truth the modern world produces
  – Hilary Jenkinson

Ella Mary Marriott Watson was nineteen years old when she was sent abroad to find a husband. She had fallen in love with a Glaswegian bricklayer called Harry, but her father disapproved of the match. We don't know much about Ella and Harry's love—except that they met in Christchurch—so let's suppose it was like any other. Youthful and ordinary, coy and adoring. But bricklaying was tough work in 1893 and Ella's father feared she would be widowed young and left in financial ruin. By sending her to London, he hoped she would forget Harry Marshall. He hoped she would find a new suitor.

Who can resist such a tide of fatherly concern? No one. And so, on the 30th of May, Ella set sail from Lyttelton with her mother and all four of her younger sisters—Elsie, Minnie, Effie and Nell.

These facts are the bones of a story and I have even verified them by peering at shipping schedules, birth records and a parish registry on a library database. But I can imagine much more than the facts concede: add muscle and tendon, facial expressions and emotions. I can bring to mind an autumn afternoon and a steamship pulling out into Lyttelton harbour. I see a deck jam-packed with people and Ella Mary Marriott Watson, tall and striking, squashed against a railing. I give her a hat to hold against her carefully pinned hair, and sense a wind that whips at the crowd. People wave goodbye at the dock below. Dense clouds threaten rain. The sea churns. Ella barely notices everyone jostling around her. Her face is pale and she wants to shake her mother by the shoulders and yell, *But what if Harry Marshall forgets me?*

Instead, she turns back through the crowd to where her sisters are waiting near the ship's cabins. They need to prepare themselves for the long, sickening trip to England.

I know this story because Ella kept a diary while she was in London. She actually kept two diaries in London, because she was sent to England *twice* to forget Harry Marshall. Once when she was sixteen and then again three years later. Nearly 115 years after these trips, Ella's elderly granddaughter Jill donated Ella's two diaries to the research library where I work as an archivist. Jill also enclosed a handwritten letter, addressed to anyone reading the diaries.

The library where I work is big and august, and it is named after Alexander Turnbull, a colonial book-collector who died in 1918. He was a serious completist. 'Anything whatever relating to this Colony, on its history, flora, fauna, geology and inhabitants,' he once said, 'will be fish for my net,' and the library continues to collect two copies of every book published in New Zealand or by a New Zealander. It is home to the most significant

Katherine Mansfield archive in the world, which means it holds not just her personal papers but her typewriter, her passport and a large skein of her hair. The library's rare books collection is housed in a special cage that can be unlocked only with the curator's thumbprint. Think: cuneiform tablets, Shakespeare's Second Folio and Milton. It's full of illuminated manuscripts, made from vellum and gold leaf, that have the weight of intention behind them. A monk's ancient concentration emanates from the pages. *Keep me forever*, they seem to say.

But alongside these blockbuster objects the library also accumulates the odds and ends of ordinary people's lives. Documents like Ella's diaries make up most of the collection. Ratty bus tickets. Postcards from Cairo sent during the Second World War. Menus, faded and stained from a life lived among meals. Memes. Tweets. A photograph album from someone's grandparents' honeymoon. Most archival documents are offcuts of the past, slivers that have survived through chance and benign neglect in attics, boathouses, garages and large messy cupboards. Documents may arrive at the library folded, stained and torn but they're readable, just—with spidery handwriting barely legible on the back.

As an archivist, professionally responsible for pampering time's debris, I have often wondered about the nature of my contract with the past and the lives that unfurl in my care. Regardless of how haphazardly they're collected, archival documents are often called the 'raw data of history'. It's a phrase that gets bandied about by the profession and one that evokes objectivity and precision. It implies we can rely on archives to draw authoritative conclusions. We want to trust archives, so we can know the unknowable (aka the past).

And according to traditional archival theory, we archivists are ciphers for this truth and orderliness—we simply turn documents and objects over in our hands. We catalogue items according to common and sensible standards, applying the necessary categories. We write lists. We aren't meant to imagine the deck of a ship or admit we bear witness to others' secrets and that we tread silently in the footsteps of strangers.

After they arrived in London at the end of July, seasick and exhausted, the Watson family rented a house at 27 Mowbray Road in Upper Norwood, a fashionable district of Lambeth that had been attracting the wealthy mercantile class since the mid-1850s. I have walked down Mowbray Road on Google Earth and paused outside the Watson family's large brick villa. From where I stood, its gabled roof reached into the sky and, in the garden, an oak tree shaded the porch.

For most of its history Upper Norwood was covered by an ancient oak forest but in the nineteenth century the ever-expanding city encroached further and further until all the trees became lumber and the lumber became train tracks, like a Victorian edition of *The Lorax*. Eventually the Crystal Palace, an enormous and showy glass folly built for the 1851 Great Exhibition, was even relocated nearby and, in its shadow, Upper Norwood cemented its reputation as destination du jour. From Mowbray Road, Ella and her sisters could stroll to Crystal Palace Park every afternoon. In early October they even saw the famous Crystal Palace cat show. *There were a lovely lot of cats,* Ella wrote, *all sorts and sizes. About three or four hundred in all. Two kittens in particular attracted my attention, like little sheep with bright violet and heliotrope eyes.* This made me smile, leafing through the pages. Ella's imagination was stuck at home, even as she was staying in fashionable London. *Little sheep with bright violet and heliotrope eyes.*

To keep the scraps of the past from the bin of today, archival practice follows two essential principles. *Provenance* instructs archivists to record each step a document takes towards the archive and note every owner through whose hands it passed. *Respect des fonds* tells us to group together material that was created together. In essence, these phrases are French for 'don't muddle things up', and they form the backbone of every single task.

When Ella's A5 notebooks landed on my workbench it was my job to enclose them in appropriate boxes and catalogue them. The first book was hardback, covered in red marbled paper. The second was covered in soft black leather. Sitting in front of me they looked like the exercise books kids use at school, with cream pages, blue ruled lines and a red margin down the left-hand side. The only giveaway that dated them was Ella's pristine cursive handwriting.

My work looked like this. Measure the notebooks and take notes: *Both 19.5 x 16 centimetres.* Make a folder to store them (specifically, an archival quality 21 x 30 centimetre four-flap enclosure made from acid-free, lignin-free 270gsm stock, in Milk White). To make the folds sufficiently crisp, you press a bonefolder—a smooth, blunt hand tool carved from a cow's tibia—along the doubled-over cardboard. Then: put the notebooks in the folder. Fold Jill's accompanying letter into a sheet of paper (archival quality, A4 acid-free, lignin-free 80gsm stock, in Buff Tan). This will keep it physically and intellectually separate from the notebooks inside the housing. Write the library's catalogue number in pencil on the outside (*MS-Papers-12038*). Add a sticker that says *Do not change the order of any papers in this folder.*

To write the catalogue record I use my brain like a bonefolder, making perfect and crisp categories for Ella's diaries, first by subject (*England – Description and travel*; *England – Social life and customs*) and then by date and format. I write a small biography of Ella, containing the facts necessary to disambiguate this Ella Mary Marriott Watson from any other Ella Mary Marriott Watson: her birthday, her family members' names, where she was born, where she lived. *Archival practice*, this process whispers back at me, *is the natural enemy of uncertainty.*

Ella had kept a dried flower pressed inside her diary, so I emailed our book conservator, a raffish, sixty-something, cowboy-booted American. *Hi!* I wrote, *I am working on a 19th century diary that contains a dried flower (!!!). The flower has already marked the pages of the book!? How should I store it?* He dropped by my workbench to inspect it and, leaning on the bench with his chin resting on his hand, the conservator exhaled. 'Well, well, well' he said.

These accidental companions—hair, rocks, seashells—that sneak into the library alongside documents give archivists all kinds of headaches. They don't belong. They're out of order. They smell like the sea. They cause a chaotic quiver because the whole building is kept aggressively clean. In the spacious, quiet workroom, pot plants are forbidden and staff can't bring food or drinks through the security doors. New to my job seven years ago, I passed the head conservator as I accidentally paraded a banana through the workroom on my way to the kitchenette upstairs. He stopped me, eyebrows raised into his mop of floppy English hair. 'What's going on here?' he said.

Conservators use phrases like 'water damage' and 'light-related discolouration' to describe how the centuries eat up pages or how foreign objects burrow in. An elegant email may read, *The paper is very brittle in some parts (with evidence of acidification), but soft and fluffy in others (where affected by microbiological activity). Iron Gall ink shows through the verso side, but corrosion spots mostly appear on the bottom half of the document. Some accidental creases.* Their near-meditative habits of attention always strike me as archival practice at its best. They are non-judgemental and curious, both about the material under their care and also the forces that try to destroy it: acidic ink, poor careless folding and grease from long-gone human hands.

The book conservator eventually made a tiny clear envelope from acid-free plastic for the dried flower. I returned it to the diary, taking care to put it between the same two pages where Ella had left it.

As July gave way to August and its stifling heat, the Marriott Watson women settled into London. Ella's three older brothers—Henry, Frank and Win—were already established in the sprawling city, trying to find work as actors, and the family's social life became giddy. Every day Ella and her sisters filled their time visiting, or being visited by, their acquaintances. The Symonds, the Kennaways, the Andrews. *I had an invitation to afternoon tea at Miss Collins' but I'd promised to go with Kitty Munro to the Austins',* Ella wrote. In the evenings, the Watson girls went to dances, concerts and supper-parties. *There were several very nice gentlemen there. We were quite a houseful and it was quite half-past two before we got to bed.* Someone was even robbed in their neighbourhood. They saw Frank perform as the villain in a play set during the Crimean War. *He was such a brute*, Ella said.

A neighbour in Upper Norwood, Miss Humphries, apparently had the Sight. Ella noted that she came over for the afternoon, and I wanted to ask: did they sit and drink tea in the cool parlour, out of the afternoon heat? I can almost hear Miss Humphries' laugh tinkle throughout the house.

'Shall I tell your fortunes?' she says.

My mind invents what the diary conceals: three good Victorian girls' opinions on fortune telling—their father was an Anglican minister after all. Ella looking at Elsie. Elsie looking at Min. Min eyeballing Ella. Ella pausing, and then abruptly dropping her hand in Miss Humphries' lap. A good Christian girl, but also a teenager.

'Oh! Don't look at me like that Min! It's not Sunday.'

Miss Humphries erupts into a giggle. Min rolls her eyes.

Later, writing in her diary, Ella will actually write down what Miss Humphries foretold.

'Ella,' she whispers, 'I can tell from your palm that you will love passionately, you will have five children and a very long life.' She shuts her eyes and exhales. 'I see extremely good luck.'

As an archivist you spend most of your workday in the company of the dead. You neatly stack their things. You tend to their thoughts. As you examine a collection, feelings pour out of hastily penned aerogrammes and pool on the workbench in front of you. Someone else's ideas briefly become as tangible as your own, their opinions moulded to the shape of your mind. In her diary Ella sometimes didn't— or couldn't bring herself to—write Harry Marshall's name. Instead she referred to him in a code called Pigpen Cipher.

I dreamt such a real dream that ⊓⅃ˉΓˉ⊀ ⊐⅃ˉV⅂⊓⅃·Ŀ·Ŀ *and I were married, in dear old St. John's. I remembered him as actually putting on the ring. I was married twice, once in walking cotton, and once in bridal array. It was so real and all the next day I felt different, as if I really had been married. I felt down in the dumps, at finding it wasn't true.*

The poor kid, I thought, as my mind filled with Ella's overflowing teen longing, as sweet and sad as bubble tea tipped over. I remembered my own dashed dreams, like how my date to the Year 12 ball had kissed my best friend instead of me at the end of the night and how, when I was seventeen, the beautiful blue-haired punk who worked at the rec centre never, ever returned my gaze. As I stood at my workbench, bruised all over again, it was as if Ella had elbowed her way through a hot, crowded supper-party, right up to my side. She peered over my shoulder at the open book. 'I always thought it would be Min who read my diary,' she said.

Unsurprisingly, archival practice is full of Pākehā talismans intended to prevent this kind of haunting: heavy gsm paper stock, white gloves, locked temperature-controlled vaults, air conditioning. It makes for a strange tension when you work in an archive long enough. We care for the past as tenderly as possible, but our inherited methods assert that the living are firmly in charge. We are supposed to enforce a boundary, seal the dead away.

The strategies for containment extend far beyond our archivist's tools and the banana-free workroom. They are enacted on all visitors. The secure reading room, where the public can read Ella's diary, is walled off from the rest of the library behind a glass wall and a locked door. It is sealed off from the aimless people just wandering around and the litters of schoolkids shedding teenage heat and noise. It is sealed off from the unhoused people who come in to use Facebook, and the woman who does Chinese calligraphy with her granddaughter. At the door, you need to provide ID and prove you are who you say you are. Inside, silence smothers the room like a pillow and, out of respect, sunlight stops itself short. If everything is quiet enough and clean enough, the past will be neat, or at least distant enough to understand. As I box up old diaries and smooth out old letters with my white-gloved hands and my bonefolder, I wonder what mess we're so afraid of. Ghosts who ask questions, probably.

I said 'Pākehā talismans' because traditional archival practice loses its stubbornness when it's questioned and dissolved by Māori archivists. The boundary between the past and the present is recognised as permeable, welcomed as such. At a wānanga in Gisborne I listened to a conservator from my work explain how to care for documents and photographs, not just physically but spiritually.

'We call them "the agents of deterioration" in the profession,' said Vicki-Anne. 'These features of the environment that *do* physically impact taonga. Dust. Light. Water. Heat. Everything we do, we do to minimise their effect.' She held up a framed photo. 'A good-quality frame with UV protective glass is one very simple way to keep taonga safe. And if possible, keep them away from the kitchen, with all that heat and light.' Then she grinned at the audience. 'But remember, too, there's only so much I can teach you because *you* know what's best for your tīpuna.'

In Te Poho-o-Rāwiri wharenui, sitting literally inside Ngāti Porou history, under the steady gaze of their tīpuna, I realised something more balanced was possible. We could do memory work alongside the dead, with their help and guidance. I quietly laughed at myself, too—this Pākehā archivist, with my Pākehā background, finally having the insight other people have practised forever. Contemplating the room around me, I wondered what it was that made me think I was qualified to care for other people's ancestors, when I didn't know them at all.

At the same time, I started making sense of my deep connection to Ella. My own great-grandmother, fresh off the steamer from England, was knocking around Christchurch only a few years later. Unlike Ella she was poor, the daughter of illiterate millworkers from Bradford, and a Quaker, but still: an urban, English teenage girl seeing the twentieth century start in Christchurch.

Throughout the autumn and into winter, Ella met a lot of young men. They came to afternoon tea and they sat in the parlour. They met her at church concerts and they walked her to Croydon. When it rained, her companion might tactfully produce an umbrella and smile down at her, his glance momentarily returned. *Mr Matson, one of the 'R.M.S. Austral' engineers, came to tea with us. He is a very nice fellow, good-looking and young. Minnie and I walked to the station with him.* Ella's cousin Kitty became engaged to a man called Dr Morris and *Dr Morris's brother Christopher was very nice.*

In the first week of January, after an icy and uneventful Christmas, London was gloomy. The lamps in the parlour had to stay lit all day and there were no letters from home. *I was most miserable, the whole time, thinking about New Zealand.* One snowy evening Mr Ryatt, a friend of Frank Watson's, took dinner with the family, bringing with him the short-lived promise of fresh opinions. Unusually, Ella's diary recounts a whole conversation from this night, but I furnish the dining room scene myself. The clink of cutlery on china. Flickering candlelight. I stoke the fire too warm and see that the conversation lulls. Mr Ryatt's cheeks have quickly flushed. Across the table, Ella's head swims, as if her family's idle conversation ripples on the surface of a lake, much too far above her head to reach.

'Did you know, Mr Ryatt,' says Minnie, breaking into a long silence, 'you remind me very much of . . . a man of our *acquaintance* in Christchurch. Harry Marshall.'

Ella's head snaps up. Her spoon clatters to the floor.

'Really?' says Mr Ryatt. 'Well, isn't that, uh, something.'

'Yes,' continues Minnie, 'in fact, he is our brother-in-law.' She smiles at Mr Ryatt with closed lips. 'Or rather . . . he is to be.'

At the other end of the table, Elsie chokes on her bouillabaisse.

'Oh!' says Mr Ryatt, eyes bulging as he swivels his head from one sister to the other.

Minnie beams at Mr Ryatt, and then at Ella. *All eyes were turned over to me and of course I went scarlet. I thought it was a very mean thing to do.*

The fact that we know what Ella thought about a dinner party in January 1894, or what she thought about anything— Harry Marshall, London, the Crystal Palace cat show—is unusual. Her interior life is an unlikely offcut because archival practice, left unchecked, only ever reproduces broader patterns of power and exclusion. The 'raw data of history' is actually a very patchy dataset. What's caught by the net, as Alexander Turnbull would say, always reflects the interests of those who wield it. At the scale of national collections, this was historically white men, and what we've thought of as valuable tends to reflect only their values and their actions. Within archival theory this bias has also been conveniently masked by appeals to universalised values. Archivists should seek Truth, for the good of Society, for example.

Ella began her diary in 1893, the same year Kate Sheppard submitted the women's suffrage petition to parliament, and, the year I worked on Ella's diary, I also joined a project to write biographies of suffrage petition signatories. We aimed to research one person from each of the petition's 546 sheets because, at the time, we had information about fewer than sixty of the 25,000 people who signed. *Let's add a few more*, we said. This proved to be a lofty goal because in 1893 most women were at home minding babies while their menfolk learned trades, built cities and fought wars. And, for most of the twentieth century, archivists were concerned with preserving the real action of history—trade and war—and men's letters about trade and war, rather than what women talked about when they were alone together in a quiet kitchen.

During the petition research we found that women were the empty centre of the doughnut around which the squishy dough of fathers, husbands and sons swelled. We'd cobble together a woman's biography but only by using a newspaper advertisement for her husband's business in the *Ohinemuri Gazette* and her son's First World War military records. Specific details about any woman usually emerged only when she interacted with the state: born, married, died. I hit the jackpot when I found a will from one woman's deceased estate. So here's something we actually know about someone called Amelia Joynt (sheet no. 26): she left her household furniture to her eldest daughter.

Contemporary archival theory is more likely to ask *Whose truth? And whose society?* And with those questions we see how, in other ways, Ella's diary fits neatly within the traditional value system of archival collections: she is Christian, Pākehā, and seeking heteronormative, though class-crossing, love. That she was sent to England identifies her even more firmly as a colonial settler, someone who directed their gaze at the centre of the British Empire. The way she created her diaries, written by her and her alone, suits an archival method of seeing the world: our main principle, *provenance*, doesn't account for shared ownership. A collection must always be derived from a single person or a single entity, like one family or one company. Even the idea that paper is the natural home of memory—over a stream, a building, the voice, or textiles—is culturally determined. To choose this document to preserve is to make one small choice about whose perspective makes the stuff of history, and archival collections are, in the end, just thousands of individual choices like this.

In Upper Norwood, Ella's winter dragged on. If I could pause on Mowbray Road outside number 27, I might see the windows shut against the biting air and hear the house groan as it resettles under a dense blanket of snow. Ella's brothers would arrive pink-cheeked and smiling after theatre rehearsal, or fresh from their walk through Croydon. Win or Frank or Henry would let himself in through the front door and call out, bringing a cold wind that blows up the stairs.

'Why the long face, Ella?' says Win one afternoon. He unwinds his scarf and hangs up his coat, without noticing it drip onto the hallway carpet. 'I've brought my latest play to read you.'

Ella tries to raise the corners of her mouth but she hasn't had a letter in weeks. The snow isn't stopping and *Win was awfully stuck on Milly Collins* and at least three times a week she and her sisters had to trudge into the dark night to dance with the Mr Labingtons and the Mr Kennaways. *In the evening, we went to Dr. Proctor's dance . . . I must confess, I did not enjoy myself. I was fearfully tired and I missed my New Zealand friends. We didn't arrive home until 2.30am.*

A few days later, the pipes burst and the house is nearly flooded with icy water. It is already an inch deep in the basement when Ella wakes to hear her mother shouting from the floor below.

'What's going on, Mother?' I hear her ask, standing on the stairs in her nightgown and wrapping her woollen shawl around her shoulders.

Her mother clatters from room to room shouting instructions at the maids, at Ella. 'We've got to send for a plumber!'

Ella slumps down onto the stairs and shuts her eyes. She leans against the balustrade, resisting her own tears yet again. *The house was in a dreadful state.*

Not long after I finished cataloguing Ella's diaries, I moved to a new team at the library and began work as a digital archivist. In this job I cared for the spreadsheets and email accounts of the dead rather than their notebooks and letters. The principles of *provenance* and *respect des fonds* still applied but the work looked different. I abandoned the stash of acid-free cardboard and I learned to code. I said goodbye to the white gloves because floppy disks were less haunted than handwriting. The work was still meticulous, though, and I once spent a whole afternoon gently scrubbing a stack of floppy disks to remove glue left by several brightly coloured stickers. With a packet of Q-tips and organic solvent, I copied what I'd seen the conservators do, moving in small circles, millimetre by millimetre.

The disks belonged to the writer and academic Gillian Heming Shadbolt. They contained her work and personal papers from the mid-1990s, though some documents might've been written by her children, seated at the same computer in the family lounge. Gillian is clearly older than Ella, already a mother and divorcée; her late twentieth-century world inevitably broader, bigger. She's drafting a book and planning research trips to England and New Guinea but the family's private life still peeks through. One letter begins: *Well, where oh where shall I start. I know I was the most hopeless letter writer that ever there was.* Gillian, or perhaps her daughter, plans the table layout at a family wedding.

I liked and admired Gillian, but I also wished that Ella's life and mine were still silently adjacent, that I could tell her there was a cat show in Kilbirnie coming up or the gossip about the policy analyst in my new team, Dave, a disconcertingly sexy Glaswegian like her Harry—hypermasc with a heart of gold—who offered me a mini-croissant in the kitchenette. 'Would ye like a pastry, Flora?' he said. I found myself willing him to use my name every time we talked about business rules for managing obsolete file formats. I wanted Ella's opinion, to know what she'd say about this Glaswegian. Maybe she'd laugh, like she did at Kitty when she was *awfully gone on a Mr Labington*, or maybe she would agree that *he is very nice* in her placid way.

Ella's diaries lived permanently in a temperature-controlled vault, buried under the pavement in Thorndon, but Heming

Shadbolt's would live in the National Digital Heritage Archive (NDHA), a vault of industrial servers holding over 245 terabytes of data in Seaview, Auckland and Palmerston North. Many archivists find digital files harder to love than maps, paintings or Captain Cook's cutlery. I sometimes wonder if it's because these objects undermine our archival fetish for uniqueness and our need for control. Tweets multiply asymptotically. Emails spew from people's fingers.

The intangible nature of tweets and emails means that they don't do emotions like objects do, either. When you hold Ella's diary you know that you're holding something she held, packed in a hatbox or perhaps hidden under a pillow. A conservator's report might say *iron gall ink on woven paper, some water damage* but all you see are her cursive words and a small blotch where the ink has run. You don't have to work hard to imagine Ella, sitting in the cold, badly lit drawing room, wiping away a smudgy tear. She looks up, you make eye contact, time collapses. *I woke up with a splitting headache. New Zealand letters came at twelve o'clock but none for me from* ⊓⌐ᖵᖵ< ꓱ⌐ᖵⅤ⊓⌐ᒷᒷ *which did not improve my head or temper.* Characters encoded in Calibri or Times New Roman seal something off like the flower in its plastic sleeve. You can't see tears spilled on a keyboard.

Sometimes, I think that this is just a failure of imagination. The emotions in a Google Doc are no less intense or earnestly felt than those secretly poured into an exercise book; they just look much flatter, somehow shrivelled, on a screen. But peer closer, past the anonymous font, and you'll sense human hands. Fingers hover over the keys and then suddenly they dive, fossicking out words, letter by letter, with thousands of implausibly deft gestures.

Last year I archived a cache of files from the early 1990s, written by someone I can't name. The documents were long love letters, typed in precise, emotionless Arial, but they were garbled and in turns rageful and beseeching, written from a woman to her married lover. The dead will always write furious letters to their exes.

By March 1894, Ella and her family have been in London for eight months. A thaw drips around them and rain strips the oak tree of snow. Bluebells peer out from the lawn. I give Ella a sunny afternoon to plant the flowers listed in her diary: carnations, lily of the valley, cornflowers. She wipes her muddy hands on an apron.

On an afternoon walk to the Crystal Palace, Ella, Minnie and cousin Kitty skip neatly over puddles in the muddy road. Their laughter still puffs steam into the air but at least they are out of the house. *Our walk would have been lovely, had it not been for three young gentlemen who followed us all the way, passing remarks and trying to get us to enter into conversation with them. When they couldn't manage that they picked up stones and began throwing them at us. This shows you what the English gentlemen are like. They are all alike in my eyes. The N.Z. mail came in, one from Mrs. Munro, Alma, and Harry Marshall. Which made me feel so light hearted and happy.*

Preserving digital paper is harder than preserving actual paper because computer files have malleable edges. File extensions are especially flimsy. The .docx or .xlsx is not actually part of a file but stored in a computer's operating system. They're tiny companions, easy to leave behind, and they fall off without anyone noticing, leaving it impossible to identify or open a document.

Inside a document the boundaries are barely more stable. A 1995 ClarisWorks file opened on a contemporaneous computer (a 1994 Macintosh Performa 6110CD) will wholly reflect the writer's intentions. Margins sit in the correct place, a **12-point sans-serif font** announces the author's ideas with authority. But open the same document with different software or on a newer Mac, and small things start to change. Margins might

shift,

the font is now **serif**, and the page numbers have moved. All this can happen just beneath your perception too, like when you scrutinise a friend's face after you haven't seen them in years, and you can't tell what's so different.

Because of their pliability, digital files can betray their authors with a creativity their hardcopy cousins lack. Ella omitted details and scribbled through words. When you delete something on a computer you don't erase it but write over it with the equivalent of a scribble. A computer system still has a record of what you wrote, buried in a backup. In the case of some early file formats, deleted data still orbits the document from which it was ejected. When a file is opened in the wrong software the logic of the tiny database fails, and its efficient pretence of secrecy falls away. Years later, scrap words or whole paragraphs appear, fossilised.

In 1993 you write a letter to your lover, a diaristic howl, and you delete your lover's name. Nineteen years later, a digital archivist opens it, trying to figure out how to render the file properly. And there, a small fossil hidden among misspelled nonsense and boring verbs, is a name.

As a discipline, digital archiving can't agree about how much this porousness matters, and we definitely can't agree on what constitutes the 'archival object', as it's called. Ella's notebook is clearly the Thing we should preserve: her words are secured to the pages of the book. But the answer isn't so clear-cut for Gillian Heming Shadbolt. More contemporary records are slippery, and the recent past an eel. Some archivists say that, given how complex digital files are, enacting *provenance* means truly caring about files at only the material level. The sequence of 1s and 0s encoded onto a magnetic surface is the only thing we can reasonably declare secure or stable, so let's focus on that. Use whatever software and whatever computer to get the stuff open. As long as we can read the information in some way—any way—why bother reproducing exactly what Heming Shadbolt saw. We're just making work for ourselves. They are ruthless pragmatists.

To others, the archival object should be as close as possible to what Heming Shadbolt viewed when she was writing. They argue margins and font are significant, that they shape meaning. We let Heming Shadbolt down when we ignore this: you might seat someone at the wrong table at the wedding. They believe in maintaining old computing environments, in caring for the digital file as if it were an artefact in a museum. They are nostalgic, heartfelt romantics.

This question has led to fights at conferences and very public beef, like it's the Informational Capulets taking on the Artefactual Montagues. For what it's worth, I am a Capulet, someone who sees the 1s and 0s as the only component we can reasonably expect to preserve, given how complex even the most basic digital objects are. If Heming Shadbolt's words are visible on any digital page, her voice is at least there, heard. It doesn't matter too much what it looks like.

As with memories and life stories, I don't think there is a single truth to a digital object. To me this makes them, weirdly, more honest than other documents. Through them it's easier to see how archival practice itself is only ever partial, and we're always drawing conclusions from a false sense of certainty about our relationship to the past or the authority of archival collections. I also like how the digital world makes me feel—as if the more you look at something, the more closely you inspect it, the more it starts to change shape and bleed into its surroundings.

At work, as I swim in the very recent past, caring for the records of late twentieth- and early twenty-first-century lives, I wonder how Ella would have recorded her life now, or what would have happened if she had fallen in love with Harry Marshall in 1993 or 2013. Who are all the other Ellas, the young women with dazzling interior lives? What are they up to?

In the coffee queue one Monday morning I chatted to Dave. He has two daughters and coaches both their netball teams.

'How'd they get on this weekend?' I asked.

'Oh terrible,' he said cheerfully, 'but that's okay. Everyone gave it a choice go.'

I smiled, pleased to know that the world contained many girls who could never ever disappoint their father like Ella had hers.

'Do you, uh, have netball in Scotland?' I asked.

'Yes we have netball in Scotland,' said Dave.

Later that week my friend Joe, slightly shamefaced, showed me a screenshot from his teenage daughter's Instagram story.

'You know that if you hold your thumb down the story pauses, right?' I said.

'Alright, alright.' Joe rolled his eyes, and then an earnest curtain drew over his face. 'But seriously. What do you think?'

Judging by the lovely snap, I thought Joe's daughter had a boyfriend, is what I thought.

Joe sighed. 'Poor kid, she's gonna hate me asking about this but, you know, I'd like to meet him.'

'Well,' I said, 'she did add you to her Close Friends list. That's something.'

Joe laughed. 'Yeah, I realise I'm lucky to be invited into her life at *all*.'

In her diary, Ella is sometimes cryptic. She says *I heard a very great piece of news today*, and then, without elaborating further, she shuts the door. You are hurtled out of her brain and back into the workroom, staring at the 2B pencil in your hand and the pile of paper on the workbench. She says, *Laura and Aileen came and spent the afternoon with us, we had a long quiet confidential chat together and I walked to the station with them, where we had to wait five and twenty mins for a train.*

'What news!' I mutter out loud, but Ella isn't around anymore. Silence shivers through the room, as if she has only just stepped outside, but definitely isn't coming back. All I can do is imagine the three of them—Ella and her real, contemporary interlocutors, Laura and Aileen Austin. They sit quietly in the living room, one of them keeping a furtive eye on the door. Later, they walk to the station, arms linked, ambling. I'm annoyed at Ella, but then think, Well, she deserves the privacy of every teenage girl.

The silence is loudest after her diaries end. The last entry marks her twenty-first birthday on 20 October 1894, before she comes home to Christchurch and before we find out the fate of her teenage love. *I had some awfully nice presents*, she writes. *A most beautiful little brooch . . . a pretty scarf.* Several blank sheets follow this, so she didn't run out of room. I want to know why she stopped writing. Did she decide she was too old to keep a diary? Or was she finally having too much fun in England to write anything down? Had she met her future husband?

It strikes me that, above all else, archival collections contain absences. Some are so small you barely notice or you think you can step over them because they're unimportant. What someone had for breakfast, the colour of Ella's new scarf, or a missing file extension. We paper over them by adding the extension back or triangulating the facts. Other gaps are much larger and to address them would require transforming the profession: entire lives and whole communities are missing. All of this is what I suspect orderliness is meant to hide, or at least soothe.

But the longer I do this work, the more gravitational pull every gap exerts: a practice born of certainty has only led me further and further away from it. According to archival theory, this makes me a bad archivist. But I think I've just found a way to interpret what feels like an emotional, if not literal, truth—a way to open my arms and enfold all the library's ghosts. I imagined my way into Ella's life because it didn't feel possible *not to* after spending so long in the company of her thoughts. I agree with the historical novelist Hilary Mantel when she concedes that 'the pursuit of the past makes you aware . . . of the dangers of your own fallibility'. Working as an archivist is the same. At the end of every day, we're left holding our white gloves and feeling topsy-turvy about our relationship to the dead and their records.

Luckily for me—and the historic record—Ella's granddaughter Jill knew how the real story ended. Her letter to the library picks up where the diaries stop. Written in ballpoint rather than fountain pen, here's something we actually know about Ella Mary Marriott Watson: *She remained loyal to her Scot, Harry Marshall, and they married when she returned. They had three children: Collin, Tasma, and Nancy (my mother). Two years after my mother's birth Harry died of diabetes, leaving Ella a widow with no money. The very situation her father had wanted to prevent. Ella became the post mistress at Duvauchelle on Banks Peninsula for some years, and later at the post office in Ferry Road, Chch. Being a widow in those days, with very little inherited money, was not easy. She met with considerable hardship.*

A Portrait of My Mother

Ah, I think, so this is autumn: the season when spiders come inside. Outside, a cold weeknight drapes itself over the suburbs, and in other people's houses I assume time is passing as it should, with gym clothes and leftovers and scrolling. But the spider and I stand still, together outside time. She'd emerged into my peripheral vision as I stepped from the shower, and scurried into the space where my husband removed the bathtub. I peer into the corner from a safe distance and wrap the towel tighter around me. Water begins to pool on the floor at my feet. I eyeball the spider. The spider doesn't move. Evening continues.

When my mother still rescued me from spiders, she could scoop them up with her bare hands. I remember those bitten nails and her freckled forearms. *Don't worry*, she'd say to me, laying her hand on the floor or in the empty tub, *they're more scared of you than you are of them*, and then, to the spider, who by now would be stepping gingerly onto her palm, *Come on, that's it*. She'd smile back at me. *Can you open the window for me please, doll?* And I would fling the window open and retreat. My mother would lean out and place the spider onto a plant. *There you are.*

Tonight her voice still wafts through my brain, like a draught that whispers *It's more scared of you,* and for a little moment I can see myself as the spider might. I am large, I am clumsy. I have so few legs. My mother's voice will always arrive in my mind, usually a quick second after my own, because she was the kind of mother who talked to her children constantly, quietly narrating the world to me, and shaping it like someone kneading dough. She seldom talked down to us.

*

Like, her rule was: if you want to play sport, honey, you'll need to ask your father to drive you. Saturday mornings were for dozing in bed or drinking bottomless cups of milky tea and reading. She read dense, philosophical novels by Iris Murdoch and Elias Canetti. There, her thoughts could splash in a pool that lay out of reach on regular days, while she taught small children how to wash their hands and played nursery rhymes on the piano.

You see, when she met my father, my mother was tiny and boyish and cute, an Ethics 101 tutor in Dunedin, all high-waisted corduroys and a shaggy haircut. She wielded her mind like a paring knife. Principled and exact. She used phrases like 'subordinate clause' and 'sufficient conditions' with ease. Eventually, she was dragged kicking and screaming (her words) to Wellington. After she got pregnant with my older brother, her PhD withered and fell away.

Not a rule but a request, spoken gently, crouched down at child height, as she buttoned up my padded jacket against the wind: 'Could you call me Vicky, please?' She explained, standing right there on the path, that 'mum' was a word people whined, a word screeched through the house into the kitchen. It was a word that engulfed women. I nodded solemnly. Also, I liked using her name and said it before all my questions, certain my mother had all the answers. *Vicky, could I please have a biscuit? Vicky, what's that tree?*

Once, on the way to swimming, I asked her, 'Vicky, what were you like when you were young?'

She didn't take her eyes off the road. 'I don't think I was half as sweet as you, my beloved. I had to leave David Washburn's 21st because I threw all the empty champagne glasses into the fireplace.'

Quiet beside her in the car and now lost for words, I couldn't imagine this version of her. I still can't. My five-foot-nothing mother, who's always trying to convince people to come aqua-jogging and who sends me photos of her cherry blossom tree. She rings her best friend's mum twice a week, to pass on news and hear what happened on *Shortland Street*. My mother's friend has been sick for months and can't face explaining—yet again—to his mum that he needs radiotherapy. But someone needs to remind Elaine when she forgets, to gently clarify what's going on.

Every day after her four kids went to school my mother disappeared into her writing room and wrote short stories. She emerged each afternoon, back into the clamour of family life, to tie herself to the kitchen and cook. Someone always whined *Viiiicky I'm hungry, when's dinner?* And, somehow, still, every single evening after the dishes and baths and bedtime negotiations were done, she found time to read me books. One year we read all the Narnia stories in a row— except *The Last Battle*. She had her reasons. Sitting on my bed she said, 'Love, pay no mind to that story. Can you see how it's not ethical? C. S. Lewis kills off Susan for liking boys and wearing lipstick.'

Once, driving me to a high-school dance, she said, 'Flordor, I don't care who you like or how much, but make sure you wait until university to have sex. Your clitoris will have a much better time.' I blushed from the passenger seat. I also remember her using a different word, one that also begins with a *c*. She isn't even sure this conversation ever happened. She might be right, but I still like to think of my mother as the kind of woman who can say 'cunt' with tenderness and care.

One winter morning, I rang my mother from my university hostel in Dunedin, homesick after only a few months living in her hometown, dumbfounded by first-year epistemology.

'I can't do it,' I sobbed. 'I just can't. I don't understand anything. Vicky, what does "synthetic a priori" even mean?' I was crouched on the floor of the phone cubby, and the other kids in the common room could probably hear me wailing. 'I hate Kant, and I'm so *uncool* here, I don't have any friends.'

'Slow down,' my mother said. 'Start at the beginning. What's this about Kant?' She sipped her milky tea. 'He's talking about different kinds of truth, my angel, and the way you acquire them. He's asking, is it reason or experience?'

I slumped back against the wall and relaxed, saved once again. Maybe I didn't hate Kant. These philosophers, they're lucky we have mothers.

It somehow came up years later, too, when I was an adult with a bathroom and weeknights and dishes of my own, that my mother had always been scared of spiders. It took all her willpower to touch them and drop them outside.

I gawked at her. 'But you never said anything.'

She shrugged. 'You were scared, and someone had to do it.'

*

The water keeps pooling and my big autumn spider heads for the door, running in the way that only something with eight legs can. I lunge into her path and trap her under the empty toothbrush glass.

'Oof, sorry,' I say, 'I'll get you out of here in a minute.'

I'm less gracious than my mother, as I address this creature I'm about to bundle outside. I leave the spider there for a minute and ferret out a piece of paper. I also need to put some clothes on because the April evening is getting cold and I haven't lit the fire yet. I decide to place the spider by the vine near the front door, something sturdy enough to hold her weight.

As I usher her out into the night, I think, Ah, so this is what it means to mother myself.

Gather Your Strength

Sometimes, a ball of dense, rubbery dough lives in my stomach. I want to say it's a human pearl, but it's not so lyrical, this pasta deadweight that presses on my organs. It's eased only by a hot water bottle or having Pat around. He's home for the weekend, so I tell him today's worrying thought. *Aw love, I'm sorry*, he says, frowning.

Every time Pat comes back from the island, I get used to his presence just as he leaves. He laughs on the phone to our friend. A new pile of seashells sits by the bathroom sink. I'm struck dumb when he touches me. My blood slows and my brain dims. The tide goes out a very long way.

The cat wakes me in the middle of the night, often twice. She spasms—dredging coughs and barks from her gut—before she vomits on the bedroom floor. Or she squirms, and then unfolds herself with a stretch because her body is always damp and uncomfortable after she's leaked piss on the duvet. Scrambling out from under a deep sleep, I switch on the lamp. We both blink in the bright light. *It's alright, girl*, I say and climb out of bed to strip the sheets.

Tethered to home, I'm knitting a jersey while Pat's away. It's made from brightly coloured scraps of wool, a way to use up the odds and ends I've amassed over years. Tessellating crosses sprawl across the garment as it grows inch by inch. The pattern is knocked off from a Gucci vest I saw on Instagram.

Every day when I get home the cat meows at me once, loud as her tiny frame can muster. She's perched on the arm of the sofa. *Hi little one*, I say as I put my bag down. She closes her eyes and I stroke her soft head, her knobbly body. *I brought you some Whiskas*. The cat is deaf, though, and can't hear my voice as I try to calm her.

I prefer my jerseys half knitted. When I'm tense, the tendrils of my mind can stroke the bundle on the couch at home. I see my hands pick up the needles and draw wool between my fingers. My blood slows and my brain dims.

On Taranga, Pat is surrounded by the ocean and the busy lives of animals. In the water, on the beach, through the bush: kororā, sooty shearwaters, ruru. The island is pest-free and tīeke swoop past his head. Once, Pat stumbled across a tuatara on the ground by his tent. It scuttled away from him and plopped into a pond. Sinking downwards, safe under a layer of water, it glared up at him as he backed away. When Pat rings me at night—*What are you up to, love? How'd it go at the vet?*—his voice is sometimes drowned out by waves or bird noise.

I like watching the cat potter about the house. There she is: gazing quietly out the back door or slinking behind a lamp. Something clunks while she explores the crockery cupboard. Her quiet soundscape of unexpected chirrups interrupts my day. I try to think of a word that means 'lovely chaos, moving slowly' to describe her. She is the gentle imperfection in the Zen garden.

While a jersey remains unfinished it leaves a tiny, shining fishhook in my spirit. When it becomes the Finished Thing it takes on the dullness of all domestic, real-world objects. It is something I could sleep in. I will probably spill hummus on it.

What kind do we think this is, girl? I say to the cat one day. I've noticed a new seashell next to our bathroom sink, rosy pink and about the size of my palm. Several ridges—the umbones, according to the internet—radiate outwards from its flat bottom edge up to the crinkled round top. I learn online that this scalloped shell would have belonged to a tipa.

On his visits home, Pat works in the garden. There he is: tending to the lawn, now digging out a shrub, now gazing at the tall purple salvia planted under the window. *What d'you reckon I do with that guy?* he asks me as he tracks mud into the living room. Leaves blow in behind him through the open door. I am sitting at the kitchen table, watching the Japanese silver grass by the letterbox wave in the wind like a tiny green sea.

Seashells, I read, are almost impossible to break. They leave fingernails, claws and teeth in their dust. Molluscs absorb dissolved carbonate and calcium from the ocean, and extrude it again, to harden on their body between layers of biochemical proteins. They gather their strength from the sea.

A few years ago, Pat built a beach simulator in our spare room. It was pieced together from secondhand shops and other people's rubbish: a deck chair from the tip shop, sunglasses and a space heater from Newtown St Vinnies. He bought two giant, perfect seashells from the David White Gallery and attached them to a pair of earmuffs he'd dismantled. *Sound like they look,* he said.

When you finish knitting a jersey, you wash it gently with warm water and baby soap, then leave it to dry, flat in the shade. This lets the wool stretch and breathe one last time. It eases with a small sigh and settles down to dry into a real-world object. My jersey—with its colourful vomit of crosses in four different greens, a mustard, all those reds and pinks and blues and yellows—lies flat on its towel. In our cramped house it's inevitably in the way. I step over it; the cat just wanders across it.

When you put the shell muffs on and close your eyes, the sea washes through your body. You hear the tide as it ebbs a long way out from the spare room.

Just before the cat finally dies, Pat drives through the night all the way to Wellington from Whangārei to say goodbye. We bring her body home from the vet and place it—silent, stripped of her meows and chirrups—on her blue-and-purple woollen blanket by the fireplace. Kissing her soft head, I am surprised that I don't recoil from her corpse, this final thing, this empty vessel. In my throat, though, a claw sticks: the sharp edge of having witnessed her life end.

I sit with the cat's body while Pat digs a hole in the garden. When he's done, we wrap her in her favourite pillowcase and place her in the ground. We are both crying. I don't know much about soil or life cycles or biochemical proteins, but I hope her body will feed the worms and nourish the trees she liked to sit under so much.

After Pat leaves again, I learn that silence changes its meaning based on context. In the morning it is a presence; in the evening an absence. In the stillness before breakfast, it might say: *You're awake, you're alive, you're alone, you're lucky.* In the dark after dinner, and in a voice of Netflix fatigue, it says: *Your husband lives on an island and your cat is dead.*

If a knitting project doesn't work it ends up in my worm farm, atop the uncanny salad of vegetable peel, teabags and eggshells. The oozing mass of worms writhes under sleeves that were too short, or a jersey knitted with the wrong size needle. They need my failed projects to keep them warm through winter and dry-ish when it rains. In return, they will graciously munch through the wool and place my thoughts in the ground.

Pat rings me one evening from Taranga. *How are you going, honey?* he says. *I'm so sorry I'm not there.* I say, *It's okay love, I think I just need to hear your voice.* I can hear him smiling down the phone. The sea roars behind him. *Well, not much has happened to me today so why don't I just tell you about all the food I ate and the animals I saw?* I hold the phone to my ear and his voice washes through my brain.

When Pat is out of reception, I try to imagine what he and his DOC colleagues are doing that day. They tramp into the middle of the island, they step through leaf mould, peer down into traps and haul clumps of pampas grass from a hilltop. At home without the cat, I have more time to tend to the little wilderness of worms, snipping up their vegetable peel even smaller, mashing up old mouldering bananas, tipping even more water than usual over them on hot weeks.

Some days, when Pat can't ring me and the worms have been fed and I have nothing to knit and the cat is still in the ground, I place the shell muffs over my ears and lie down in the Beach Simulator.

I will the sea to rush through my body.

Proust Yourself

1. A madeleine

Newtown New World is way less evocative than it used to be. The owners are doing a big refurb, and, except for when they installed the self-checkout machines in the mid-2000s, it's the first time anything seems to have changed in the shop. They're replacing the interior in well-organised chunks. First, cream floor tiles gave way to sanded concrete. Then tradies stripped out the yellowing ceiling to leave a lofty dark space and exposed ductwork. The walls and shelves have been painted a chic black. After years of my local supermarket remaining exactly as I always imagined, something now looks different every time I pop in. Last week I snapped a photo of the old industrial lino sticking out from the chiller: cream with flecks of red, grey and blue, soiled from the scuffing decades of Newtown's sneakers and boots.

People love to tell me that Newtown New World is the most expensive supermarket in the country, to which I usually pull an ugly, sceptical face. I love Newtown Mall because it was where I first rode in a trolley as a toddler, swinging my chubby legs and clutching a slice of luncheon sausage. I knew Newtown New World before I knew the days of the week, when I spent most of my life sitting on my mother's hip as she lived life one-handed. She would carry me around like a wriggly sack of potatoes all day while she made my three older brothers' lunches, chatted to other mothers outside their school, tidied away toys, talked on the phone to her friends and bought milk. Now, the new supermarket adds friction to my memories. In an unfamiliar space I have to work harder to remember.

After photographing the lino, I leaned over the frozen foods chiller and peered at the TV dinners, all those inviting cardboard boxes branded with 'plant based', 'abundance' and 'natural', superimposed over glossy photos of warm mushy meat and cubed vegetables. I was looking for the brand Super Snack, specifically their shepherd's pie, which I hadn't eaten since I moved out of home at eighteen. But I couldn't see a single one, not next to a pile of Wattie's Classic Macaroni Cheeses or the Weight Watchers Beef Bolognese. I settled for a Wattie's Cottage Pie because it seemed similar enough.

'Do you think it's okay to do this?' I asked Pat at home later, as I read the description on the back of the box. *Homestyle mince and vegetables with a tasty potato topping.* I turned the oven on to 180.

Pat raised his eyebrows and tried to suppress a smile. 'I think you're fine, babe.'

'Yeah, true, I won't be stripped of my vegetarian badge for one cottage pie, eh?' I slid the pie into the oven before I could chicken out. 'Besides, apparently I only need to eat a little bit for this to work.'

'Watertight plan,' said Pat.

For weeks, or maybe it was months, an empty space in my memory had been bothering me, like a splinter in the palm of sense-making. I needed to act.

And if this worked for Proust, maybe it would work for me?

In his book *The Art of Time in Memoir*, Sven Birkerts devotes a whole section to Marcel Proust. Birkerts wants to explain to would-be memoirists how memoir operates, to help them write elegant literary prose about their own lives. For Birkerts, the seven volumes of Proust's novel, *In Search of Lost Time*, and Proust's writerly story are so central to the practice of life writing, so edifying in the best methods for shaping narrative pots from the clay of everyday experience, they're now cliché.

The most instructive incident happens early in the first volume. One morning Proust is given a little French biscuity cake thing, a madeleine, which he idly dunks into his drink before taking a bite. And 'suddenly the memory revealed itself. The taste was that of the little piece of madeleine which on Sunday mornings . . . my aunt Léonie used to give me, dipping it first in her own cup of tea.' Proust is incredulous. The bite was everything. 'The sight of the little madeleine had recalled nothing to my mind before I tasted it,' but now lost memories flood back. Proust's Aunt Léonie emerges, his nightlight, the nursery walls, and he soon has access to whole chunks of his childhood he had forgotten, 'an entire vanished world'. For Proust, our most potent and meaningful memories are hitched to our senses. Untapped, they can hide for years but then explode from a wee biscuit and overwhelm you.

Good food writing understands this. Sneakily, it's never really about the food but about the relationship between food and the sensory world. A meal is a vessel for the senses: it slices into the white noise of your mind when nothing else can. I love Nina Mingya Powles for this quality. In her book *Tiny Moons* she describes a year of her life in Shanghai, as experienced through all the sweet watermelon, pineapple and plums she ate, as well as every variety of freshly made pancake, dumpling and noodle she found: boiled, fried, in soup or out, in soy sauce or sesame oil, the smell of meals mingling with blossom trees and car exhaust. For Powles, food is both map and compass in a city where she feels caught between loneliness and comfort, because she's moved back to Shanghai in her twenties after living there as a tween with her family. She captures that impossible quality of eating, like when you fall in love, of being both extremely grounded and totally transcendent. She is of the world and outside it at the same time. It's hypnotising to read. Even watching someone else methodically prepare food—whether her mother or the local jianbing-maker—allows Powles to absorb the city, her past and her memories, and to partially reconcile the sometimes irreconcilable: who you were and who you've become.

I am comforted and elated by this kind of stance, of seeing the world and everything within it, writer included, as permeable. The lines between objects blur, past and present cloud in the water, the literal and metaphorical put down their cudgels and shake hands. If only I could listen and look at the world like Proust or Powles, the possibilities for understanding might be infinite.

What to make of the summer I turned sixteen? The years around then, the early 2000s, are confusing partly for logistical reasons. My family was coming and going a lot, as domestic stability unfurled into something more complex and contingent. My father had moved out in the late nineties, quickly followed over two more years by my oldest brothers, Henry and Rufus, when they started university.

That summer my third brother, Humphrey, and I were still living at home, but as teenagers we were simmering at that age when you're trying to shake off your family by spending more and more time 'out'. In November, too, just before our NCEA exams, our mother had committed herself to an in-patient psychiatric facility in Dunedin. For a while, as the evenings got lighter, Humphrey and I lived alone, clunking around in the empty house. Eventually Henry and Rufus came back to Wellington to spend the university holidays living with us.

Just after my mum left, her friend Pip brought round some raisin cake and sat beside me at the kitchen table, scrutinising my face from under her blunt, grey fringe. Though I didn't know it at the time, this was to be the first of many raisin cakes because Pip brought us baking every weekend my mother was away. This is the only one I remember but I am sure they all would have been equally warm and delicate. Near buttery.

'Your mother's not crazy,' Pip said. 'She's just very sad.' I wanted to meet her eyes and nod, to show my understanding, but somehow the nod melted away each time I tried. Luckily, I didn't have to speak because my mouth was full.

Pip looked at me gently. 'She just can't look after herself, let alone you or your brother anymore.'

I am not entirely permeable it seems because my memory quits discreetly at raisin cake and questions arrive like office temps. My mother must have left, and Henry and Rufus must have come home. But who drove her to the airport? I didn't have a licence. What was it like when my brothers came home? I can't seem to remember even the most basic administrative details, like—what did we do for money? Who did all the cooking? What did we eat?

'God, probably endless Super Snacks,' I had said to Pat, after it struck me how much I didn't remember.

'Super Snacks?' he said, looking up from his book.

'Only the best frozen meals in New Zealand,' I said. 'They were my favourite. Me and Humph ate them after school, like lasagne and shepherd's pie and stuff. Mince city.'

Pat turned back to his book. 'Man, I had to eat carrot sticks after school. We didn't even have a microwave.'

Pat grew up in the country, twenty minutes' drive from Waipukurau. His mother mostly fed them from an abundant, well-maintained veggie patch and they had a house cow called Rocket and a gang of bantam chickens.

I laughed. 'You were probably too busy milking Rocket.'

I thought about trying to write some cute images to represent this absence, but I couldn't think of any that rang true. I can't say that this part of my memory is like an empty ice-cream container or the wrapper after you've finished your Subway. It's not a quiet lake at dawn or a dried-up river bed.

Where my brothers should be sits a pristine void.

When I pulled the cottage pie out of the oven, crouched in its pert little black plastic tray and clear plastic wrapper, it was steaming. The hot mince, all caramelised and bubbling slightly around the edges, was mostly hidden underneath a melty cheese and potato topping. I let it sit for two minutes, eyeing it from the table, before peeling off the plastic and digging my spoon into the slush. As I closed my mouth around the instant potato and brown meat I leaned back into my chair and shut my eyes. Soon a cottage pie apparition would rise before me. Not anyone's Aunt Léonie, but maybe one of my siblings or even a version of myself. Seconds passed in expectant silence.

I opened one eye, then the other and found my adult life still thrumming around me. Kitchen bench. Dirty dishes. The toaster. Disappointment landed on my shoulder, like a big unwanted parrot. Looks like you can't Proust yourself, I thought, dropping the spoon into the plastic tray, where it slopped mince onto the table.

I called out to Pat, who was tinkering with his bike outside. 'Baby, do you want to finish this?'

His face appeared round the front door. 'Oh, yeah? If you're done?'

Proust coined the phrase 'involuntary memory' to describe his biscuit method. It's the way the past sneaks up on us fiercely, the way the body stores what the conscious mind hasn't. To tell a story using involuntary memory allows you to sidestep factual ordering and arrange your experiences into an associative pattern. You can, for example, place today's kitchenette coffee alongside the coffee at your grandmother's wake and the coffee on your dentist's breath. Through this you illuminate a greater, more essential idea than a simple timeline of events would allow. You find meaning in that which previously felt meaningless.

Proust contrasted this with 'voluntary memory', which is a shrivelled and systematic 'mechanical retrieval function', based on unearthing receipts or your calendar. It has real spreadsheet energy. Birkerts writes, a 'patient focus on preserved materials will bring back troves of specific information—what we ate, what we paid—and we could write the account of our lives in that fashion', but that picture of our past would remain flat and procedural, the opposite of emotionally charged. Only memories in a thick emotional sauce, like chicken drumsticks marinated overnight, will offer up true insight.

Lying on the couch later, a bit sheepish, I thought, Maybe I'm just an un-mystical person. I needed to accept that I chase the past using judgement, inference and deduction rather than letting it come to me in cooler, unbidden ways. I had to concede to Birkerts that I've staked a lot on voluntary memory—it makes my salary, even. If archival practice has only one big idea, it's that memory must be verifiable, exhumed from letters, diaries and photographs, rather than divined from snacks. This would be seen as an unreliable methodology for generating understanding. Archivists demand evidence and corroboration from paper. We'd throw away the madeleine but keep the recipe.

Although, in our defence, it's also an archivist who'd be able to tell you that Proust's madeleine started out as a piece of toast in the early drafts.

2. Voluntary memory

I was six when I started keeping my own records, motivated by felt-tip pens and an instinct to write things down. My diaries overflow from a carton in the hot-water cupboard. My very first entry in 1993 reads: *Daddy rang. Everything's fine.* Where was my dad? I wonder now. I can't tell if there was a causal relationship between these two statements or if they are just side-by-side observations.

By the time I was fifteen, I meticulously accounted for my days: *School was boring today because hardly anyone came.*

Sarah was sick, so was Lily. Gina didn't arrive until social studies.
Thanks to voluntary memory, I want to say a little defensively,
the past rings clear as a bell across two decades. I find it very
hard to read, though. Immediately after cataloguing who
was at school, I described in detail how it had felt to wear a
G-string for the first time the weekend before. I got *skanked
onto* more than usual at a party. I hypothesised that somehow
the boys knew I was wearing sexy underwear.

There, I want to slam the diary shut and fold myself
under the ground.

And yet. If I pause for a moment, curiosity itches at me.
Man, I went so hard on the diary writing. I filled page after
page with idle thoughts. It must have taken hours, and it
reads like a written response to the empty time of childhood.
All that boredom. In the years and months preceding my
mother going to hospital, I catalogued every school day,
weekend and party. I transcribed movie dialogue, novels
and MSN Messenger conversations. I reflected on my
friendships, what I ate, where I went and who I saw. In order
of preference, I listed my favourite bands, songs, books and
outfits. More than anything, my diaries are full of boys. The
boys I liked, the boys my friends liked, the boys we didn't
like, the ones who didn't like us. *Sophie was rapt cos she found
out Angus still likes her. I was talking to this guy named Daniel
at a table and our knees were touching under the table.*

Buried in this scree of burgeoning heterosexuality, I
provide only tiny glimpses into the unravelling adult world
at home. At thirteen I noted, *Vicky is really unhappy, she cries
all the time and isn't happy. If I had a wish it would be for
Vicky to be happy. If I had three wishes they would be 1) that
Vicky could be happy 2) that I got a really nice boyfriend 3) no
further wishes as yet.*

Only one small sentence in November 2002 speaks directly to what's going on: *I have to try and pass NCEA while my mother is in a nut house. Fuck it, fuck it all. It makes me angry. And it doesn't make me cry. I just don't care anymore.*

If reading my diary isn't like dunking a madeleine in tea, maybe it is like smoke creeping under a door. NCEA. Vicky. These are ordinary nouns that curl into the air. Awareness begins to unfold in my brain. Wellington's spring wind. Snippets of a phone call with my eldest brother Henry, unusually solemn. *I don't think it's a good idea for you to visit her, Flor.* Memories hatch.

When my mum was first admitted to hospital I was about to sit my English exam and I was preoccupied with correctly identifying the 'themes and/or key ideas' in Katherine Mansfield's short story 'Her First Ball'. I wanted to become a novelist, so supposed I should pay careful attention to Mansfield's technique, but, sitting at my desk, my mind couldn't make the connections I knew my teachers expected. When I looked at the words on the page I couldn't see underneath the plot. A girl went to a ball, danced with a bitter old man. And . . . ?

On my way home from the exam, I ran into my friend Ishan on the bus. His parents ran the superette and I liked chatting to his mum when I bought milk. I was fond of Ishan too—he was smart and loyal, ringing my friend Lily up week after week and taking her to the movies. *Lily's going out with Ishan AGAIN oOoOooo.* I flopped down next to him and smiled.

'Hey! Howsit going?' I said.

'Hey—yeah good.'

We talked about the relief washing through us now exams were done, and what we'd do at the weekend to celebrate. But then Ishan paused and looked at me.

'What's up with your mum?' he asked.

'What?' I said, trying to hide a flinch.

'The other week she spent ages at the shop—she seemed kinda lost? My mum didn't know who to ring.'

This was unwelcome news, broadcast by someone I wanted to impress. I prayed he didn't know she was gone. I forced myself to roll my eyes, trying to mimic how my friend Jess talked about her mum when she 'fussed'.

'Huh, yeah, she's so weird.'

Ishan spluttered into laughter alongside me, reassured. 'So weird, right?'

Luckily my stop arrived before I had to say anything else.

There it was again. Another conversation that gave off the new, dismaying whiff lots of conversations had seemed to recently. I'd noticed that my English teacher cocked her head when she asked how I was and, for weeks before my mother went away, she and her friends had been falling quiet when I walked into the room. My own friends seemed increasingly confused when I mentioned anything about my family. It was as if the frequency of my life emitted a high-pitched whine I couldn't hear, though I was beginning to realise other people could.

Over the last few months even I had started finding ordinary things curdled with discomfort. Every afternoon, when I got home from school, I'd stand outside the front door not wanting to turn the handle, sometimes for minutes. I did this so often that in my mind's eye this period of my life evokes the front door of our house and the small brick porch. When I stepped inside, I'd start translating what the silence meant, ears pricked. It was a new silence, you see—so unlike my loud clattering childhood. I'd gently push open my mother's bedroom door, but every time, luckily, she was just asleep. I would retreat as quietly as possible, to heat up a Super Snack in the microwave.

And then, before long, came all those raisin cake months.

After his exams ended, Humphrey got a summer job working at the New World bakery, and with our mother away the house was now constantly quiet. I was home alone a lot but I don't think I minded. I found a part-time job at Whitcoulls in town and our weeks settled into a new rhythm. On Wednesdays and Saturdays I put on a polyester uniform and tidied shelves. Behind the counter I gossiped with the three other teenage girls who worked there, as we all tried to make eyes at the one skinny uni boy on staff. The only person who was above making eyes at Danny was my favourite workmate, a smart and wry goth from the year above me at school. She and I would walk home across the city in the twilight, laughing about ditzy customers and wondering whether the 2IC was stealing from the till. (He was.)

I'd been babysitting a little girl who lived down the road every Monday night for a few months too. Poor Izzy. I always made her plain pasta for dinner, sauce plopped straight from a Wattie's can onto chewy penne. We usually just watched Cartoon Network until I tucked her in. She sometimes forgot herself and cuddled up to me, sucking her thumb. Mostly though, she would remind me that I was much less fun than her last babysitter.

I'd make a face back at Izzy's furrowed glare, her knees all akimbo. 'Oh yeah?'

Apparently, the old babysitter always brought round special boardgames and baking. Sometimes she drove Izzy to the movies.

'Sorry,' I'd say, laughing, 'but I don't know how to drive.'

After Izzy went to bed, I'd watch *The Powerpuff Girls* with the sound turned down or do my homework. Lily would ring me too, even though we'd just seen each other at school, and we'd talk about what we were watching on TV or who we were messaging on MSN.

In December, I told Lily where my mother was.

'Like, how bad is it? Is she okay?' asked Lily. 'Have you talked to her since she left?'

'Not really,' I said. I was standing in the lounge, fidgeting at a plastic truck with my foot. 'She told me she won't try kill herself, though.'

Lily was quiet down the end of the phone.

'That's something, right?' I said.

'Yes. I mean . . . well, I'm not sure,' Lily conceded.

I walked around the lounge talking to Lily, picking up Izzy's toys and dropping them into the toy box one by one. I wanted her parents to think I was a decent babysitter, even if Izzy didn't agree.

I didn't tell many people where my mother was—just Lily and our other friend, Jess. Or rather, I think I must have told Jess because I can visualise her, scrutinising me as we walk along Evans Bay Parade on a sunny afternoon.

'I thought something was up,' she says. 'I wondered why there were never any adults at your house.'

My brother Rufus didn't tell anyone where Vicky was, either, choosing instead to tell people that she was in England visiting her sister.

*

On weekends my friends and I would descend on whichever party we'd heard rumours about. One Saturday night in January a classmate's parents were away in Melbourne and her house bulged with teenagers. In our Glassons halter tops my friends and I danced in the living room, practising our body rolls and singing along to the chorus of 'Hey Ma', hoping the boys would notice. Jess was the only 'hot' one of my friends, the only one who could pull off a credibly come-hither body roll and she'd just lost her virginity to her boyfriend. She and I were friends from French class and spoke in what our teacher called *franglais*. Jess was hotter than the rest of us because she had a membership to Les Mills, which we also pronounced the French way, *les mills*.

After Cam'Ron finished on the stereo, we collapsed, tipsy and too warm, onto a couch.

'Alex was very good *dans lit*,' she said.

I envied Jess and her apparently seamless admission into the world of sex. The rest of us seemed to flounder; our awkwardness burned just a little brighter.

Much later in the night, as people started to pass out or filter home, I dissolved into a puddle of tears at the foot of a staircase. I didn't know what to do with my arms during a body roll. My mother was too sad to look after me.

'Taaaaxi!' a boy yelled, bounding past.

Another voice said, 'Some girl always cries at the party, aye.' It seemed to belong to the pair of baby-pink Skechers and bare legs teetering out the door. I kept sobbing.

But then someone else—and I don't know who it was— shouted after them, 'Won't you fuck off! She's just sad!' Whoever-they-were sat down next to me and wrapped an arm around my shoulders.

*

Other Saturdays, when I didn't go out, I might be woken by a tapping on my window and a voice hissing in the dark, 'Flordor . . . FLORA. Oi—let me in. I've lost my keys.'

I'd stumble out of bed, scurry through the downstairs laundry and let in whoever it was, either Henry or Rufus. One night one of them, I can't remember which, tracked blood all through the bathroom after a fight.

'Thanks Flor. Love you,' they'd say, giving me a fuzzy hug, before stumbling to their own rooms.

While my mother was away, Rufus and his friend Simo got arrested for jumping the fence into the Basin Reserve, trying to take a shortcut home. Simo rang up at four in the morning from the police station and I answered the phone.

'Oh, hey, um, Flora?' he said. 'Can you get your brother? I really need to speak to him.'

Henry, probably bleary-eyed and grouchy, ever in charge, drove to the police station to pick them up.

On Sundays, the one day without school or parties or work, my life seemed to slow down again. A steady, ordinary beat thudded through the world, low and clear. I slept late, cuddled up to my tatty stuffed giraffe, then ate Marmite on toast and slurped milky Milo in bed.

In the afternoons, Humphrey and I were usually invited to our friend Caleb's house. Caleb's mum would heat up chicken nibbles and sometimes even let us drink her Diet Coke while Humphrey, Caleb and I played Nintendo for hours. Slouched on the huge squishy couch in their lounge, none of us needed to say anything, except to debate tactics for *The Legend of Zelda*. We fell into hysterics one day when Caleb laughed so hard that green jelly, bright and chunky, spewed out his nose. It wobbled on the carpet while we yelped *ewww!* and Caleb prodded it with his foot. We couldn't splutter out any words, for laughing so hard, when his mum popped her head round the door to identify the racket.

And then, I guess, on Mondays the week would begin again, again and again, every week until my mother could come home.

3. *Asking Around*

As an adult, I can't stop thinking about what the early 2000s must have been like for my mother. All those months, she felt her life dissolving around her and she couldn't stop it. I've only properly remembered people outside my family, the friends and strangers who peeked in momentarily at the confusion I thought I was doing a good job of hiding. What was it like for my mother? I want to know.

'Truthful or tactful?' she said when I asked. My family always said this when I was growing up. If you asked someone for their opinion—on a meal you'd cooked or your outfit or to check if you'd said the wrong thing—they'd always reply with this question. Do you want the truthful answer or the tactful answer?

'Truthful,' I said.

'I remember feeling like my whole life was black,' she replied, 'like I lived underground or at the bottom of the well. But when I looked at you and Humph, you were bathed in a golden light. You waved at me from above, and I needed to protect that for you.' She looked at me, smiling a little bit. 'I think you only rang me once while I was away?

You were so upset because you couldn't understand that Katherine Mansfield story, with the dance and the mean old man who says women get fat arms as they age.'

I didn't remember the phone call, but I did remember how much I hated not understanding 'Her First Ball' and how much I wanted Katherine Mansfield to get in the bin.

'What was weird,' she continued, 'is that *I* had read the story once and knew to tell you to focus on how it *ends*, you know, to help you get it. And after we hung up, I remember thinking, That was a good day. I did something good today. I was far away, had let you down, but could still be your mother.'

'Jesus, Ma, you didn't let anyone down,' I said. 'That whole time was so much worse for you.'

We sat in silence for a second before I asked, 'Do you remember much of it?'

She grimaced slightly. 'Yes.'

Maybe, then, I am just missing something fundamental from Proust's recipe. Because if this method is concerned with recovering the sensory nature of your old life, what do you do if that sensation is numbness?

The whole time my mother was away I nursed a very cold and very still feeling that spread from my stomach outwards, through my limbs and into my mind. As I experienced it, there wasn't anything obviously overwhelming about this numbness. It didn't arrive with any sensation other than that of cool distance, as if I sat behind a pane of glass in my own life. My mental image of talking to Pip over the raisin cake is framed like something from TV. In my mind's eye I see the two of us chatting from the other side of the room. I don't register Pip's kind expressions from where I saw them at the time, sitting on a chair beside her. My memories aren't there because they probably didn't have sensations to attach themselves to; they slid off the ice rink in my core.

One thing I do know is that this numbness morphed into a single very powerful and blunt conviction: I was special. I was better than other people because I could tolerate the circumstances of my life.

I felt weird and a bit guilty about this for years until I confessed to a therapist in my late twenties that, as a teenager, I thought I was better than everyone because nothing could upset me. She looked at me over her glasses, across the room, in what felt like a very pregnant pause. But then she just suggested that this might have been an understandable coping mechanism for a child.

'I've never thought about it like that before,' I said.

I plucked up some courage recently and asked my brothers directly. I messaged all three of them and asked what they knew about the last time we'd all lived together. Maybe they remembered something I didn't. What was the vibe at home? my message read. Did we hang out together? For a few days they were silent—not left-on-read silent, but thinking silent. Eventually, I got emails or messages back from them that confirmed something I should have expected: they didn't remember anything either. Are you sure I was living there too? asked Rufus. Humphrey asked, Was it during the school year or over the summer? Henry said, Sorry flor, looks like we all have the same lacuna.

None of us, then, can provide an account.

Maybe I don't want to know, either—not really. When my mother came home from hospital, Humphrey and I met her off the plane at Wellington Airport. We drove her home in Rufus's little green hatchback, silent through the streets of Kilbirnie. She was smaller than I remembered, and much frailer. Her smile was taut and a lot of her hair had fallen out. In the doorway, she burst into tears. 'The house smells like rubbish,' she said.

In the absence of evidence, I think I will imagine that my brothers and I did the best we could with our ordinary youthful resources. While my cottage pie experiment failed, the TV dinner was actually still quite yum. Ten years of vegetarianism hadn't dimmed mince's light, apparently, and as I looked about the clean, quiet, tiled kitchen of my adulthood it suddenly felt conspicuous in its distance from the sticky, loud, wooden kitchen of my childhood. There, someone was always running or jumping, or talking too loud or burning toast. If I contemplated the aftertaste of instant mashed potato, I didn't feel fifteen but maybe younger, as if I were about to trip over abandoned school bags and PE gear that never made it to the washing machine. From an otherworldly swimming lesson, the tang of chlorine emanates from my warm body. I trail around the supermarket after my mum, telling her stories about school. She listens patiently, nodding.

A few nights ago I spoke to Humphrey on the phone. He'd just put his two kids to bed, and I could almost see him flopped onto the couch in his living room, exhaling briefly before he did the next thing. *Tidy up abandoned school bags. Unload the dishwasher. Feed the cat.* I was perched on the side of my bed, phone cradled on my shoulder, folding washing.

'I think I only saw you cry once that whole time Vicky was away,' he said.

'Really?'

'Yeah, I'd made stir fry for dinner. You walked in and were like, not stir fry again. And then you started bawling. Right there in the kitchen.'

I winced. 'Oh my god. How ungrateful. I'm so sorry, bro.'

Humphrey laughed. 'Well, I think I made stir fry every single night. It's all I knew how to cook when I was seventeen.' He paused. 'I mean, to be fair, it probably wasn't about the stir fry.'

'Well, that's true,' I said, and then thought: it was *stir fry*, not Super Snacks.

I heard a small kerfuffle down the end of the phone. Humphrey's daughter needed to be escorted back to bed. I could imagine him ushering her down the hallway. '*Goodnight, honey. I love you too,*' I heard him say, before the sound of her door being firmly shut.

'I'll tell you something, though,' Humphrey continued, walking back down the hallway. 'Since all that stir fry, I haven't been able to eat Chinese five spice ever again.'

Dekmantel Selectors

Thursday

As the airport minivan rattled into Tisno, Pat dozed on my shoulder and the town revealed itself to be a seaside village, cute like Meryl Streep's island in *Mamma Mia*. I felt empty-headed after only four hours sleep on our last night in Berlin, as if someone had taken my thoughts and thrown them into my pack with my togs and sandals. I stared out the window and tried to unearth all the sea-blue words I never needed back home: cobalt, cerulean, turquoise. Tisno needed other colour-words too: terracotta, bleached white, cream.

'Do you think Croatia will be like the Netherlands?' I said to Pat.

He opened one eye and looked up at me. 'You mean, all those giants?'

The Dutch countryside had seemed full of them, everywhere we visited. Wandering arm in arm through the lush, famous gardens we strolled through too. Sipping iced coffee at the shady cafés where we escaped the thick afternoon heat. Swimming at an outdoor pool where we ate ice blocks sitting on our towels. There, surrounded by tweens, we'd laughed at how short and stocky we both felt: two brown-haired goblins with Celtic ancestors, dwarfed by even the leggy European children. It had been the very beginning of our trip, then, unravelling the Netherlands together in our little team of two.

Now, as I looked at Pat in the minivan, I could tell that even his hair was growing lighter. All those weeks of sunshine. At the pool it had fallen around his face in damp dark curls, his mouth still sticky with whatever a Dutch Fruju was called. Now, six weeks later, as he dozed, hungover, his hair was chestnut.

'Yeah. Giants. Who love techno,' I said.

At his Airbnb Ben opened the front door into a shaded, cool room bulging with our friends. He grinned and waved us inside—*hi hi hi come in come in*—before rounds of *hey you guys! what's up? how was the flight?* rippled across the room. I threw my arms around everyone—even Holly and Jacob and Ben, who we'd just seen in Berlin. They smelled like cigarettes and sunblock.

'Ivan's sent us the menu,' someone said, addressing us from the huddle around the dining table. Most of the supply work was already done. Ben, with a Berliner's nous, had conjured a phone number—Ivan's. Suddenly, my head no longer felt empty, but wired.

'Has, uh, anyone met this guy?' I asked the room. No one answered. Apparently not.

Everything you could order was identified by an emoji: a horse for ketamine, glasses for speed, leaves for weed, a puffy white cloud for coke. We were to put the exact amount of Croatian kuna in an empty cigarette packet and WhatsApp

Ivan when we were ready. He would tell us where to be and at what time.

'Oi, how much K do people want?' Ben's voice rose above the distracted chatter. Most of us hadn't seen one another for years and we were all over-excited, talking at breakneck speed. But the chat would have to wait. People began doing complex deals.

'I'll buy a couple grams of K for us four but does that mean I can have some of your speed?' one friend suggested.

'Hey—is anyone getting any coke I can get in on?' someone else asked.

Pat and I couldn't agree on what we needed. 'Should we get some weed too, just in case?' he asked. 'Even out all these uppers?'

'This is . . . a lot,' I said slowly. I'd never considered taking quite this many drugs before and hadn't expected such a WhatsApp smorgasbord—or at least, had never seen this part of the process. But what else was I expecting? I didn't want to seem unchill. 'Yeah, sure, okay.'

My insides twisted a little when I imagined Ivan. Slick and leather-jacketed, silent and mean. He probably had a gun. I wanted to talk to Pat about it alone, because he'd have a good, safe read on the situation. In Liège, when our Airbnb was evacuated, he'd been calm enough to notice that the buff Belgian firemen leapt out of their fire engines and greeted one another with petite, deft air kisses. *We are very far away from home,* he'd said. But now Pat was across the other side of the room talking to Ben.

With an uncomfortable squirm, I reminded myself that people like Ivan were the *exact* reason we were here. The argument was easy to rehearse: as well as being exotic, warm and beautiful—the stuff of good parties and travel stories—Croatia was part of the EU, which made it easy for travel from Western Europe. But Croatia didn't yet use the euro and one euro equalled seven kuna. So, compared with Berlin, we were paying next to nothing for the drugs.

Luckily for me, meeting Ivan seemed like a task only the boys would have to do, a small test of masculinity, northern-hemisphere style.

An hour later, after losing paper scissors rock, Ben went to meet Ivan and the rest of us went swimming off the quay in a big splashy gaggle. Holly, treading water, laughed alongside our friend Louise. Louise had just fallen in love back home. This winter trip, for her, was supposed to be the beginning of a move overseas but she'd now booked a ticket home again. Pat, Jacob and a few others lay on the stone pier, idly passing a vape between them. I tried to get my bearings as I bobbed about, scrutinising the beautiful stone buildings rambling down a distant hillside.

Friday

Pat and I were staying at the Garden Resort with Holly and Jacob, in a big block of two-room units. Butter yellow. By mid-morning, I'd already closed the windows against Croatia's engulfing heat and thumping bass drowned out the cicadas. Down at the beach a DJ stationed on a raised concrete platform in the sea presided over a pool-party-cum-nightclub. People danced on the sand and in the water, wearing sunglasses and wet togs, while they yelled above the techno at each other in German, Dutch, French and English. Others paddled around on inflatable flamingos or mooched through the water draped over pool noodles, drinking beer.

The Garden had been built in the eighties as a holiday camp for employees of Yugoslavia's state oil company. It was now privately owned by an English party entrepreneur, a gruff Brummie called Nick Colgan, but something surface-level Soviet persisted. Metal handrails. Squat concrete buildings. All encircling a tiny golden beach like an amphitheatre.

When we'd arrived, Colgan himself demanded we leave our passports at the front desk. 'No passport, no entry,' he'd said, dismissing our protests with a shrug. Pat and I shared a look, then handed them over. Around us other partygoers leaned against their suitcases, waiting to hand over their passports too, texting and cussing because they'd forgotten to bring a hat.

People weren't allowed to bring food or drink from Tisno into the Garden, either. Every time we entered the front gates two security guards ferreted through our bags, tanned young men with buzz cuts and collared shirts. They refrained from speaking English and spent the day sitting on their folding chairs in the shade, chatting and chain smoking, so it was impossible to know what they thought of the festivalgoers who invaded Tisno every summer. The Garden hosted back-to-back dance music festivals for three months of every year and the guards, as well as the bar staff, were the only locals allowed inside the resort.

Food providers onsite were supposed to cater for everyone. You could buy instant noodles and chocolate bars from a small superette or order pizza from a terraced restaurant, where a line of people ran out the door all day. We mostly ate Gummibärchen from the huge bag Holly had smuggled in from Berlin, or kebabs from the food truck parked near the main bar, an open-sided hut optimistically thatched to resemble a tiki bar.

One feature of the Garden lived up to the name, though. Fig trees, sagging with ripe fruit, dotted the resort all the way down to the beach and no one except Holly seemed to have realised you could reach up and eat from them.

'These are so yum,' she said, with a fig in each hand. I laughed. This spirit was something I admired about Holly, and had done since university. In her, an eye for detail married an eye for mischief—or maybe it was more like she saw the joy embedded in tiny risks. She wielded these habits gracefully. Around Holly, queues for clubs just seemed to dissolve and short-cuts appeared across parks. She'd even got teeny bottles of vodka into the Garden, stashed under the lining of her handbag, without raising the security guards' suspicion.

Dancing at the beach party that afternoon, she whirled and stomped in the sun. She grinned every time she caught my eye.

'Have you and Jacob found travelling together hard?' I asked her. We'd lost Jacob and Pat but found Louise as well as another guy, a sweet-natured friend of Ben and Jacob's who lived in Leipzig, for reasons I never found out.

Holly shook her head in time with the beat. 'Not really, this is definitely not as stressful as moving to Berlin was. Have you and Pat?'

I nodded, blushing. 'Yeah. We kept shouting at each other on the autobahn.'

Driving on the 'wrong' side of the road through the Netherlands, Belgium and Germany had felt like weeks of Formula 1. Exhausting. We both flinched every time a truck whooshed past or yet another Audi overtook us with a honk. Pat had to concentrate so fiercely he'd scrawled an arrow on his hand in thick black Vivid to remind him to stay right.

As navigator, I stared into my phone but succumbed to the cliché of not reading maps very well. Pat fumed when I missed a motorway exit and I barked back at him. Cologne's one-way system reduced me to tears. We hadn't had sex since Liège.

Holly inhaled her vape and patted my arm with her free hand. 'The autobahn really sucks.'

Pat and I had eventually devised a game called 'Tricky Lefts and Sneaky Rights' to remember the European give-way rules and to make driving together tolerable. The rules were simple: shout 'tricky lefts and sneaky rights' every time we needed to turn.

Before long, Holly and I lost Louise and the Leipzig friend, but then we found Ben, waving at us from the kebab queue. And so, the afternoon progressed—losing people and finding them again, our dancing momentum interrupted only when we hurried back to our room to ferret for more sunblock or K or Gummibärchen.

On Friday night we went to the only nightclub in Tisno. Barbarella's Discotheque was easy to miss in the dark, a brick corral crouched in a scrubby carpark just beyond town, but when we arrived after midnight we were ready for magic. Inside, wheeling lights showed stop-motion snippets: people dancing, tumbling, sweating, shrieking in red, purple, blue, as if we were all moving through syrup. Because it had no roof, Barbarella's was billed as 'the legendary outdoor club where you dance and enchant under the stars'. Nick Colgan owned this too and here, like at the Garden, you could only buy beer made by the brewery he also owned in Zagreb.

Barbarella's magic had felt passionately real when we arrived but later, as dawn tiptoed in around me, I registered something of the school basketball court about it. The pavement under my feet, a wire fence. Crunched up plastic cups and beer cans strewn everywhere.

As the crowd thinned, I noticed my vision threatening to split into two, like a fish slice down my brain, and I had to concentrate hard to give myself two arms instead of four. Since the early evening I'd drunk a few mini vodkas and snorted quite a lot of K from a wonky chopping board. On the dancefloor we'd ferreted out bumps of speed from a baggie using a room key. In this way, we could keep going for hours.

I paused, to stop my reverential buzz from slipping, and then felt the world stir and thrum around me again, a thousand hands and elbows propping me up. I didn't know where the others were, so I was relieved to be with the Leipzig friend. He chewed mint after mint, shouting at me above the music.

'Hey—do you like your job?'

'Yeah, it's full of weird stuff and—'

'How did you meet Pat? He's such a cool guy.'

'At a party at Jacob's flat,' I shouted back, staring in slow-breaking wonder at Leipzig's white singlet as it changed colour in the lights. He kept talking.

'Hey—have you heard about Miles and Sapphire's break up? Fuck man, it wasn't Miles's fault, you know. Everyone's *saying* it's his fault, but he did nothing wrong—like, *nothing* wrong.'

'Is . . . your, uh, tongue way too big for your mouth?' he said, suddenly agitated. 'Mine is. Gross.' He peered at me in the dark, blinking non-stop, mouth furiously working. 'You know, you're really good to talk to.'

I didn't know what to answer. The first time I took MDMA I'd danced in the lounge at a New Year's Eve party and shivered with anticipation as my body rushed upwards.

Properly high later on, I caught myself snuggling into an acquaintance on the sofa, telling them *I love you. You're so important to me.* Almost immediately my brain whispered, *Liar.* On a regular day I knew I found this person kind of difficult and boring. As the night became more unhitched from reality, I felt only more and more dishonest, desperate to remain tethered in the normal world.

Eventually I stopped understanding Leipzig's questions and I let his words unfurl over me like incoherent surf. I focused on dancing, which at this point was more like trying to keep my balance as I swayed in the lurching, hot crowd.

Saturday

On Saturday, we swapped the beach party for a yacht called the *Argonaughty*. It was, unashamedly, a party boat. A world-famous German house DJ played on the lower deck and hundreds of people squeezed aboard to drink prosecco, boogie, shriek and sunburn. We would dance and enchant on the waves. The *Argonaughty*'s crew ran the bar, administered first-aid and unblocked the toilets every half hour, swearing quietly in Croatian. I swigged prosecco and peppered Ben with questions about his love life. He grinned at me, happy and pink, until something caught his eye.

'Hey, um, you might want to look out for undercover cops,' he said. 'Captive audience and all that.'

'Jesus,' I said, trying to follow his gaze, 'how will I know it's them?'

'Don't buy any drugs that are too easy. I mean, at worst you'll get taken to the cells for a night and you'll have to pay them off. But still . . . easier not to, I guess.'

'How much?'

Ben shrugged. 'One hundred, two hundred kuna? It's like twenty-five, fifty New Zealand dollars I think.'

'I guess everyone needs to make a living,' I said.

I was beginning to respect Tisno's hustle and everything the locals wrestled back from the marauding festivalgoers. I was even increasingly impressed by Ivan's clever business model, how it relied on hearsay, burner phones, encrypted messages and variable meeting points. All conducted in a second language, all without sacrificing efficiency. Executed at scale, the service remained secure for Ivan and convenient for his clients.

Ben said he'd even arrived punctually, pulling up into the dust on the side of the road in a recent-model black BMW, a reassuringly sensible ride. He leapt out, all ease and smiles and early-thirties professionalism. *Bok! Hello!* In his T-shirt and jeans Ivan was indistinguishable from Ben, except that his cropped hair was blond. They shook hands. Two young men sat in the back, screening text messages and filling orders. A bored young woman sat in the front seat, idly scrolling her phone. She didn't look up and it was all over in less than a minute.

In the queue for the tiny bathroom a few hours into our voyage, I gazed at the cliffs floating by, all dusty greens and browns. To my right, a young American vomited overboard.

'They've goddamn run out of beer,' he slurred at no one in particular, wiping his mouth, and then, 'Whoa. Can you see those dolphins?'

I looked out and saw two sleek grey dolphins frolicking in the sea less than twenty metres away. Me, the American and another man peeing overboard nearby were astounded.

When the news made it to the dancefloor, everyone cheered. Several people hugged.

I'd lost Pat on the dancefloor almost immediately. One second I was dancing next to him, and in another a high stranger turned around for a blistering heart-to-heart. I indulged the stranger because I'm too nosy not to but when I turned back, Pat had been swallowed by the crowd. I was sure he'd only just been there, bopping and drinking, giving me the occasional fuzzy smile. I swivelled my head around the crowd. Well, I guess I don't need you either, I thought.

Back home we never seemed to spend time with each other at parties, either. What we wanted from our nights always diverged. I wanted to dance and squawk in the living room but Pat sat outside, smoking cigarettes and talking. Glance into the garden and you'd see him laughing or gesturing with his hands. We'd come together when it was time to leave. I'd sidle up to him and he'd slip an arm around my waist. His eyes might be tell-tale bright, pupils huge, but he'd smile at me and stub out his cigarette. 'This us, baby?' On the way home he'd be chatty and excitable; we'd feed each other titbits of gossip from our corners of the party.

Sometimes, though, at the end of the night he was silent. I'd wander up to him and he'd look at me with dull eyes, emptied of some Pat-like essence I couldn't put my finger on. But he'd go through the motions: he'd stub out his cigarette, look through me. 'This us, baby?' In the Uber I wouldn't be able to draw him out. He'd go somewhere I couldn't reach him.

Much later, as the *Argonaughty* slowly sailed back to port, Holly and I were approached by a middle-aged man wearing an upside-down visor, sunglasses and pants with a high-vis stripe down the side. He materialised from nowhere, elbowing through the crowd and proffering a palmful of what looked like big red multi-vitamins.

'Pills . . . drugs . . . pills, for you?'

I shook my head and squeezed Holly's hand in the growing twilight.

'Drugs . . . for YOU?' he repeated, stepping towards us.

I shook my head again, and Holly and I turned away, trying to get other people between us and him.

After the *Argonaughty* docked I found Pat amongst a gaggle of our mates on the pier. 'Hey,' he said and reached for my hand, 'Where'd you get to? I was looking for you?'

I shucked off his hand and shrugged. 'Nowhere.'

Sunday

After we woke up on Sunday afternoon, the four of us decided to search out food from Tisno. Groggy, I wasn't too sure when I'd eaten my last kebab. Was it last night, or the night before? I'd definitely eaten some Gummibärchen and a few figs after the boat party. We meandered along in the glaring sun, gazing at the sea through our sunglasses. The road was empty. The locals were too smart to be outside in the middle of the day.

Nothing was open in Tisno except for a bakery and the superette. Nauseated and indecisive we walked backwards and forwards between them, unable to decide what to eat, until a fight broke out between me and Pat.

'Could you just choose for me? You should know what I like,' I shouted.

'Could you decide something on your own *for once*?' he snapped back. 'Why am I always in charge?'

'You?' I said. '*You?*'

I stomped out of the bakery. Holly and Jacob looked uncomfortable.

Standing in the sun, my ire slunk under guilt. It really wasn't Pat's fault we were both strung out. It had been a very big night—weeks of very big nights, really. I'd lost count of how many days in a row we'd been drunk or high, even before Croatia.

On our last morning in Berlin, before our flight, I'd cried all over Pat on a fold-out couch at our friend Elliott's apartment. 'I can't do this,' I said. 'I'm exhausted. I can't face more nights of partying. I don't want to take any more drugs.' He looked at me with a soft expression. 'You don't have to do anything you don't want to, love.' I can't remember what I said—probably nothing. I'd gone to bed on the fold-out couch early, dropping hints that Pat should come too, but he'd stayed up with Elliott, laughing and drinking until four in the morning. Their merry chat left me scratchy and restless. *Pay attention to me*, my brain mewled at him. And now somehow I was crying and he was awake, hungover but pert enough, damp from the shower and ready for five more days. *I want us both not to go*, I remember thinking. *I want us to want the same thing.*

As I waited outside the bakery for Pat, hoping he'd still bought me a croissant, I overheard two Australians complaining about Tisno's tiny bottle shop.

'Fuck man, I swear the prices went up yesterday. They are trying to fucking shaft us. That's cracked.'

'Yeah man, next time we should call them out and be like, we know what your tricks are.'

'Yeah, we should, like, refuse to buy anything for more than ten kuna.'

They sounded like the warnings I'd read online, written by angry tourists who'd stayed in local houses. Apparently, locals would try and get money at every turn: *Croatian landlords aren't keen on you bringing anyone back and sometimes insist you pay to have a mate round for a beer.* But I didn't blame them. The Croatian landlords were probably just protecting themselves against the bill for cleaning puke-stained carpets.

When we reached the Garden's front gate, eating our eight-kuna croissants in silence, the security guards stopped us, gesturing at our handbags. I handed mine over and they weighed it, holding it in two hands to see if it felt right, then fossicked through and found the heavy object: sunblock. The younger of the two very young men grinned at me and handed everything back.

'*Hvala,*' I mumbled.

When they did the same to Holly's handbag the weight didn't match their expectations and they spent a painful few minutes searching through it until one of them found the hole in the lining. He stuck his hand through and pulled out three mini bottles of vodka. He raised his eyebrows at Holly and grinned, no more or less agitated than he had been by my sunblock.

'No,' he said, 'no,' and waggled a finger. He dropped the mini vodkas into a large bin, where they made a loud clank as they landed on hundreds of other mini vodkas.

Holly laughed and nodded. '*Hvala!*' And then, as we walked back through the gates, 'Oh well, it was worth a try.'

'RIP mini vodkas,' I agreed, glad for the small distraction from my sour mood. 'At least we gave bottle-shop guy some more money.'

Holly and Jacob wandered back to the room holding hands. Pat and I trailed behind, still not talking.

From the beach that evening we saw seagulls wheeling in the sky above the *Argonaughty*, freshly docked after another party voyage. Her crew unfurled industrial hoses to wash a slick film of spew, beer and prosecco from the lower deck. On the mainland, the Garden's staff were erecting a huge white marquee.

When the rain set in after dinner people squealed and ran for cover. Water poured off the marquee and puddles lapped at empty chairs in the pizza café. Waves sloshed over the jetty and the *Argonaughty* rocked in her moorings. Caught by the wind, overflowing bins went sprawling. Rubbish whirled everywhere.

'Ivan isn't texting people back,' one friend announced that evening. Rumours were flying. He was injured in a knife fight. The police finally caught up with him. Someone snitched and he skipped town. Without Ivan, people walked around on edge, sodden, eyeballing each other. *Do you have any drugs? No, do you? No.* There were still two nights left and no one wanted to risk falling asleep.

Stuck inside our room, our friends tried to eke out what was left of the supply. Jacob's UE Boom was dead, too, so all we could hear was everyone's breathing and the rain growing heavier outside. We crowded around the table, elbows in each other's ribs. Across from me, Pat kept trying to catch my eye.

'Hey—that line is *way* smaller than the others,' Ben hissed. 'You gotta do this fairly.'

'For fuck's sake, I'm getting there,' said another friend. 'Do you think I'm trying to scam you?'

'I'm just saying, man—'

'Guys, can you please chill out?' said Louise.

'You do it then!' two others shouted at her. I wanted to slink away or maybe melt into the floor.

We eventually voted Holly the most trustworthy, with the steadiest hand for sharing out the drugs, and we sat in silence, watching her perform her surgery. She handed the chopping board around the table.

'Actually, I think I'm all good,' I said.

'No worries,' she replied, and then, like a conscientious host: 'Ben?'

Later, inside the big white marquee, we couldn't hear the thunder over the music, though lightning bolts illuminated the steam rising from the crowd. I danced holding hands with Holly and we disappeared into the dense, repetitive techno. We couldn't stop dancing even if we wanted to. I wasn't even deterred by the sweat flying off the stranger on my other side. Ben stumbled around happily, having made his peace with everyone.

'Sorry man, I . . . I . . . really love you, okay. OKAY?' I heard someone slur.

Pat swayed somewhere in my peripheral vision, smoking and cackling with Jacob. He'd abandoned trying to talk to me and I hadn't ever actually apologised for being snippy at the bakery.

In Berlin, my distress had peaked after I'd been bounced from an infamous daytime party.

'Not today, ladies,' the club's bouncer announced, resting her hands inside her vest. I slunk away. With my bad German and seersucker shorts, I hadn't done a good enough job of convincing her I was fun. Our friends already inside the club left in solidarity and we decided to keep at it for the afternoon, until other clubs opened after midnight.

We sat in a park for hours as afternoon turned to night, drinking and trash talking, our speech rising as we got higher and higher, faster and faster on the pills we'd swallowed. But for me, MDMA's speedy rush never exploded into bliss. Night-time made me cold and under the streetlights my friend's faces were reduced to grinning teeth. Lit cigarettes floated in the dark. When the Leipzig friend started bantering with a group of drunk Englishmen passing by, I wished he wouldn't. They looked so . . . sweaty. To tune them out, I turned to a friend's old flatmate who was explaining that smoking DMT with his dog, The Metatron, was his favourite way to relax. 'It makes me feel grounded,' he said. A few people debated The Metatron's potential star sign and then what Disney princess she channelled, but I was just desperate to check that The Metatron hadn't accidentally gotten high too. I was besieged by images of a labradoodle on a bad, sickly trip.

'Jesus. No. What do you think? That I blow smoke in her face?' said the old flatmate. He jumped up to find a toilet, leaving the conversation to swerve again. Everyone else seemed at ease with our incoherent chatter but I couldn't get words out or join in. How is this actually fun? I thought, before chiding myself: What's wrong with you? You're not here to judge people.

'I might go home,' I eventually whispered to Pat's back. He peeled himself away from another conversation. 'What's that, babe?' he said, and I noticed that he couldn't focus on me properly. Black pupils. White cheeks. Fuck, I thought. Fuck. It was two in the morning, my phone was dead, and I didn't know where we were or how to find Elliott's flat. While everyone else took another pill and packed up, jolly and excited, I wanted to cry. Pat proffered his phone, indicating he'd stay with me. *Don't touch me*, I wanted to snap. Instead, I rang Elliott while eyeing Pat anxiously. 'Can you please get us an Uber to your place?'

I was worried Pat would throw up in the car but he merely rested his head against the leather seat and shut his eyes. At home he fell onto our bed, asleep before he hit the pillow.

'Uh oh, I think someone's greened out,' Elliott said, laughing.

I wished I could laugh too but nothing came out.

'You alright?' said Elliott, peering at me over his cigarette. 'You seem jumpy.'

Eventually I lay down in bed too and gazed at Pat's sleeping form. Curled up beside him I could at least focus on his gentle breathing and lay a hand on his back. I've slept next to this body so many nights, I thought.

God, I hated last night, I wrote in my diary the next day. *I felt over-socialised, anxious, trapped and gross.* In the park, I'd sensed something newly dangerous unfurling, more high stakes than my usual interior battle about getting high. It seeped outwards, sticky like tar. We all—me, my husband, my friends—behaved so differently when we were on drugs. Our words slurred, our eyelids drooped, our smiles became floppy. Eventually, we spat when we talked. Then we repeated ourselves, slowly, yet somehow confusion still thrived. I couldn't expect people's usual responses or trust that our gestures would remain mutually intelligible. Reality had shifted towards miscommunication and disorder, and I wanted to claw it back. I also hated feeling this alarmed around Pat, who, on a regular day at home, was my source of comfort and safety. The dread had somehow transferred to him, as if he were the dangerous one, and I couldn't unpeel it from his skin.

Monday

A sign appeared outside the main bar: *No beers! No wine! DON'T AKS US!* The bar staff, with nothing to do except pour soft drinks no one wanted, faced mounting anger from punters. A woman in a bikini and sarong screeched, red-faced, over the bar. Behind her, a squad of people intermittently shouted *yeah!* like her hype men. Someone started a chant: *Get us beer! Get us beer!* With their arms folded over their white polo shirts, the staff appeared unmoved. Luckily, by this late in the festival, most people were too strung out or vacant to care that the Garden had run out of alcohol.

Tisno's official tourism website was enthusiastic about the Garden and its guests. Beside a panoramic shot of the town, squished between crystal-clear azure ocean and crystal-clear azure sky, it encouraged people to seek 'vacations with a musical background' because they can 'delight your senses'. Nick Colgan conveyed a similar message, too, evoking the Garden as the centre of a Croatian holiday-with-music, not a hermetically sealed fiefdom. 'Partygoers will spread their largesse,' he reassured us in an interview online.

So far, my largesse had extended only to Ivan, the bakery, the superette and the bottle shop.

That night, as the rain began to pelt again, the door slapped open and Ben arrived. There was a new Ivan. 'He's called Susan,' he told us. A collective exhale escaped.

'Susan's prices aren't as good but it's better than nothing, and he's onsite at the festival, too.'

This was Ben's second attempt to find a new supplier. He'd been given a dud phone number (Ivan's) in the afternoon by a pair of Austrians.

'I tried to haggle,' Ben went on, before he flopped onto the bed in the corner of the room, rubbing both temples with one hand. 'I said Ivan's prices were better—I asked why he was charging so much more.'

Susan had just replied, in a cut-glass British accent, 'And who's Ivan?' He'd dead-eyed Ben. 'Keep asking questions and my prices get higher, okay?'

Where Ivan seemed to take customer service seriously and had presented a glossy, comforting image of security and professionalism, Susan operated in the sphere of opportunism. He arrived when people were too desperate to bother haggling. Apparently, Susan's motorhome was full of people draped over the furniture in varying states of consciousness. There was money and baggies everywhere.

The morning after our disastrous park night in Berlin, I'd left Pat asleep and gone to the Bode, an obscure and unfashionable museum holding mainly coins and Byzantine art. Inside its quiet and cavernous rooms, my breathing slowed. *Pallas Athene schützt einen Kunstschüler vor Neid und Mißgunst.* I pronounced the titles of artworks aloud, enjoying the texture of German on my tongue. This is a much more pleasant way to lose my mind, I thought, peering at a seafood cornucopia carved entirely from smooth white marble. The life-size pile of thick, scaly fish, lobster and fruit looked so real I expected it to smell. I laughed, joyous at the absurdity of a stone stingray holding a bunch of grapes in its mouth. At the museum café, the barista let me speak remedial Deutsch to him. He replied slowly and gently.

After the Bode, I visited the Stasi Museum, where I stood inside a reproduction of the Ministry for State Security's kitchenette and felt the DDR rendered absurd and pitiful: the state's terror apparatus was reduced to small kitchens, office politics, bureaucracy, endless admin. The famous bugging devices looked amateur, embedded in flowerpots, picture frames and lampshades. There I could view the past with distance and clarity, a problem safely contained, so by the time I met my friends again for drinks in the twilight I was calm and peaceful, my thoughts orderly.

The night before, and my sudden fear of Pat, was forgotten.

On Susan's supply, everyone's mood improved. I'd decided to see out the night without drugs again, but I sat with everyone in our unit while they waited to take their turn on the small toilet. It was the same ritual every evening: the drugs kicked in like a cup of strong coffee, and the bathroom was so poky that even I banged my knees on the sink when I used the toilet.

'Man,' I said, 'I've never accidentally seen so many of my friends pooping before.'

Holly erupted into giggles. We sat with our backs to the bathroom door, but it was only frosted glass, and when I went to the mini-fridge I caught a glimpse of Ben's silhouette as he scrolled his phone on the toilet.

The boys disappeared early in the night to smoke weed, unable to tolerate how skittish they felt after so many days of uppers. The plan backfired only when the hallucinations started, trapping each of them inside their head.

'I gotta go to bed, babe,' Pat muttered, when I finally

went looking for him. 'I'm way, way too high.'

I flinched, but then stopped myself. I thought of the Bode Museum and speaking slow German and Belgian firefighters and air kisses and Pat in the sunshine at the Dutch swimming pool. I stroked his arm. 'Hey. I love you. So much,' I said. It was also easier to keep my dread at bay when I wasn't high myself.

'Oh man, I love YOU so much,' he said, wobbling slightly.

Late in the night (or was it early in the morning?), Holly and I danced on the beach to dark and ambient techno, in a crowd lit up red under huge, towering floodlights. A tiny chill breeze whipped sea spray at us. Eventually, she grabbed my elbow and pointed to a man with waist-length brown hair perched on a banister over the sea. He looked even younger than the security guards.

'There's Susan,' she whispered.

I scrutinised him while I did my techno two-step, watching as he talked to a guy selling nitrous oxide. Nos Guy jiggled from foot to foot and pulled three canisters from his bumbag, cracked them one by one and dispensed the contents into three balloons. He handed the distended balloons to Susan, who took them but also shook his head: *I'm not paying.* Nos Guy tensed, then gave a stiff nod and walked away. Susan inhaled each balloon slowly. Though he then shut his eyes and swayed slightly, he didn't giggle. Susan's poker face clearly went deep. You know what—screw you, Susan, I thought. Outwardly, I just averted my eyes in case Susan caught me looking at him.

After seeing Susan, I didn't think Ivan had been injured in a turf war. I also didn't think he'd been hauled off by the police. Disappearing was just the last trick in his professional repertoire. I was pleased that he'd got the better of everyone and left us to suffer Susan's mean caprice and the Garden's drought. I wanted someone, *anyone*, from Croatia to get the better of the party circuit, to undermine us marauding travellers. I imagined Ivan driving his BMW down the winding coast road away from Tisno, smoking a cigarette. His girlfriend throws the burner phone out the window. The two boys in the back are counting thick wads of kuna.

'Uh oh,' came Holly's voice suddenly in my ear.

I followed her gaze. A very wasted guy near us was struggling to concentrate on a palm held out at eye level. He took a big red multi-vitamin from a man wearing an upside-down visor. The visor man erupted into a grin. His other hand snaked around the wasted guy's wrist.

'Oh man, let's go,' I said, grabbing Holly. 'I gotta pee anyway.'

When I crawled into bed beside Pat later, he rolled over and wrapped his arms around me. 'This is still super intense,' he muttered. He could see wild colours and textures whirling in the dark room above his head—first a flock of birds, now a wild climbing plant, all shapeshifting in response to the bass thumping in from outside. He didn't seem distressed though. 'I'm kind of enjoying this now,' he yawned. 'I feel safe cos you're here. Let's go home, aye? No more tricky lefts.' He trailed off, nearly asleep.

Maybe that was all it was, then. All those tricky lefts and sneaky rights. The rhythm of our relationship was simply muddled-up by Europe. The only thing wrong was being on the wrong side of the planet.

Tuesday

I woke up early on our last morning at the Garden. Later that afternoon Pat and I would catch a bus to Split and begin the long trek back to Aotearoa. Pat, Jacob and Holly were still asleep, so I tiptoed outside to sit in the sun on the verandah. The whole resort was covered in a thick duvet of glittering stillness. There was no music, and I could hear the gentle repetitive swish of the sea. Louise was already up, reading her book with her back against the wall. I sat down beside her and put my head on her shoulder.

'Shall I tell you about the hike I did in Albania?' she said after a few minutes, while I yawned and blinked in the sun. Unlike me, Louise was well-travelled and had spent the last three months alone in Eastern Europe.

I nodded. 'Yes please.'

She had hiked in northern Albania, right up to the border with Kosovo. Her walk wound round and round mountainous woods, like something out of a fairy tale. But at the top of the hill, where you could see for kilometres in every direction, she reached a bunker. Someone in the nearby village told her that it was where the army used to stare down the wooded hill into Kosovo during the war. She'd had to stick to the track because there were still landmines in the forest.

After Louise finished her story, we talked about Ben, who was going to Zagreb after Tisno to visit the city where his grandmother was born, and we talked about our own complex families and being homesick.

'Can I borrow your books about the Balkans after we get back to Wellington?' I asked. 'I know next to nothing.'

We sat in the sun in our pyjamas. I thought about waking the others but then decided I'd let them sleep.

Down on the lawn by the tiki bar, the Garden's staff arrived and started to empty the cans and glasses from overflowing bins. A seagull cawed in the sky. They had two days' break before the next festival started.

Julian of Norwich

She decides to spend her last day walking through the narrow streets of her city, slowly and deliberately. Each foot in a simple leather slipper, one after the other through dirt and mud, her gown becoming heavier with every step. She knows these streets inside out because they've kept her company since she was born: the pile-up of human life, the mush of activity, the shouts, the mud, the pigs, the smell that clings to starched white linens hanging from upstairs windows. Rotting food, shit.

Several chickens scatter as she walks by the midden. [God wishes us to know that he safely protects us in both joy and sorrow.] She stares back at two fat old men outside an inn, the kind of men who gnaw gristle and belch. She can't remember why she used to avert her gaze. [I was filled with eternal certainty, strongly anchored and without any fear.] By the evening, the cream hem of her dress will be dark brown with Norwich.

The plague crept through the city when she was a very young girl and, for a time, Norwich was quiet and still. Bells tolled for the dead and she was kept indoors, day in, day out, squinting from the upstairs window at the street below. A body was carried past on a stretcher. A stray dog picked at food scraps and trotted on, drooling. Months later, the carts piled high with bodies would trundle by. Inside, Julian's mother burned sage and it drifted through the house, cloying their noses and eyes. Julian would stand on her bed, try to get her face closer to the window.

But today it is different. The putrid smells and the noise of the street can enter her body like music. [A supreme spiritual pleasure in my soul.] Norwich wraps around her like a cloak, and when she stands on the riverbank the wind carries the scent of onion weed and mud. Bobbing in the shallows, a duck preens underneath its wings. *Goodbye river*, Julian murmurs. The church is a stone's throw from the Wensum but her cell will face away from the water, towards the north.

I have read that Julian only just exists on the historical record, so to draw conclusions about her life people extrapolate from her two untitled theological writings—'The Short Text' and 'The Long Text'. They are two different versions of the same work, the 'Long' being a revised version of the 'Short'. These works are also sometimes published together and titled after their subject matter: *Revelations of Divine Love.* Hers are the earliest works we can conclusively say were written by a woman in English.

Untethered to literal facts, Julian's life still floats freely. She was born in 1342. She was born in 1343. She was taught by nuns. Girls weren't educated. She was a mother. Her children died in the plague. She never had children. She was named for the church where she lived. Many women were called Julian in fourteenth-century England, actually. Untethered to literal facts, my imagination wanders easily.

*

Julian died three times. Her first death was her rebirth. She died when she was [thirty and a half]. [I asked for this sickness in my youth, to have it when I was thirty years old.] Decay stole around her body like smoke in the dark bedroom she shared with her mother and pudgy demonic hands stroked her flushed face. *Join us*, they murmured into her hair. [My mother, who was standing with others watching me, lifted her hand up to my face to close my eyes, for she thought I was already dead.]

When the priest arrived to administer the last rites, he ducked through the doorway and paused. He saw that Julian lay very still in the bed, so as he approached, he started chanting and waving the cross over her sweating face. The room darkened even further. The fire in the hearth turned black and only [an ordinary household light remained], though it emanated, strangely, from the priest's cross.

And then? The thin membrane between spirit and matter truly dissolved. Christ on the priest's cross wept bloody tears onto Julian's bed, real and fresh and vivid like herring scales or rust. At this, Julian's sickness and suffering were hewn from her body. She arose, healed. And she knew that this— this—was Christ's nature, that he loved her as a mother would a child. [These revelations were shown to a simple, uneducated creature in the year of our Lord, 1373, on the eighth day of May.]

Her second death would be her symbolic death. She died when she was thirty-one. In St Julian's church by the Wensum she [the one-to-be-enclosed] rests in the western corner under the eaves. The clerks chant [pray for her], while the choir replies [pray for her].

Meanwhile: the priest's ritual. Place a cross upon her body and pace around her three times. Sprinkle the holy water. [Pray for her.] [Pray for her.] After she is raised up, the one-to-be-enclosed treads barefoot down the aisle towards the altar, every step leading her further from earthly concerns, slowly, deliberately. *Goodbye wind. Goodbye river.* The leather slippers now belong to a girl she met sitting in some hay outside a workshop. Two burning candles are placed in Julian's hands because [she should burn with love for God]. *Enter into thy chamber, shut thy doors upon thee*, says the priest, and Julian keeps her eyes shut. Her tears will not arrive, neither blood nor salt and water. Place the candles into the altar.

Finally, Julian [the deceased] is led to her last rest. She steps across the threshold and lies down in the shallow rectangle etched into the cell's stone floor. She feels the damp dirt at her back. [Here shall be my repose for ever and ever; here shall I dwell for I have chosen it.] The priest casts holy water around the grave and sprinkles dust onto the prone body at his feet. He says, *In obedience see out the remainder of your life*, before touching a hand to Julian's still-closed eyes. He steps out. The heavy wooden door swings shut behind him. Julian will barely hear the local masons when they start bricking over the cell. They will bring with them a reverent and unusual quietness, unused as they are to working inside a church.

Inside her cell Julian exhales. Slowly the smell of candle smoke leaves her nostrils. She opens her eyes and looks at the ceiling.

Her third death would be her earthly death. Julian died when she was seventy-seven. Julian lived until her seventies.

*

Sometimes, I imagine what it would be like to become an anchoress and how truly impossible it feels to remove yourself from a world that hammers on your door in the middle of the night. What sickness did *I* ask for in my youth? I'm thirty-four and eight months old and, if it were me, I would begin my last day by sitting down on the sofa and retrieving my phone from my pocket with a small, deliberate flourish. In a matter of minutes all my apps would be gone: Twitter, Instagram, TikTok, Facebook. I would then walk the streets of Wellington giving a single solemn nod to everything and everyone I passed: *goodbye sea, goodbye pigeons.* Finally, in the afternoon I would drive to Bunnings Lyall Bay to buy a thick sheet of plywood and a hammer. *Goodbye shops. Goodbye surfers.*

Once home, I would nail the wood across the inside of my bedroom door, hitting each nail deliberately, one at a time. I would lie down on my bed and close my eyes. I would exhale.

My Mother's Daughters

In the dim auditorium some of the students had fallen asleep, lulled by the twinkle of dust in the projector's beam. Someone beautiful with a cropped fashion mullet nodded once, twice, three times, and their head bowed over folded arms. A young man in a T-shirt that read *C'est la life!* chewed his nails and gazed off into the distance, far beyond and through the PowerPoint. From the lectern Mark cleared his throat. Beautiful Fashion Mullet started awake. C'est La Life blinked and returned from the astral plane to the auditorium.

The students were in their honours year at Massey University, taking a paper that examined 'photography's engagement with the "archive" as a cultural repository'. I was about to discuss personal digital archiving practices, to get them thinking about their SD cards and Instagram accounts as archives. Even digital photographs need care.

Mark, the photo conservator, threw out occasional questions to keep the class awake as he explained historic photographic processes. 'Who can tell me the base layer of a silver-gelatin print?'

A girl with Baby Spice pigtails raised her hand. 'Paper?'

'Exactly right,' said Mark. 'And what about the light-sensitive particles?'

Baby Spice looked thoughtful. 'Well, that's the silver immersed in gelatin, isn't it?'

Mark beamed. 'Wonderful. Next, we're going to talk about wet collodion glass negatives'—he gave a small laugh, clicked the PowerPoint forwards—'and baby photography.'

On the screen, a fuzzy black-and-white infant gazed back at us from the 1860s. Wide eyes. Ruffled gown. One hand balled in a little fist. The baby had moved during the long exposure and one of her chubby arms seemed to dissolve, like a small stray cloud. Nearby, her mother sat holding her steady at arm's length. The woman's hair was pulled back into a low bun, her face set in concentration as she leaned backwards out of the photo.

Mark gestured at the most important detail: we could see only the mother's head and shoulders because her arms and body were almost entirely obscured by a large blanket. Now the audience seemed much more alert. Baby Spice and Beautiful Fashion Mullet were holding hands. I smiled into the dark.

'Having access to photographic negatives is the number one joy of working in an archive,' Mark said. 'Here we see that baby is kept still under the blanket by her mum. This was a common technique in the nineteenth century. The women were always cropped out of the final shot, though—they're meant to be absent from the "official" record. But since the library has collected the original negative we see the image as it first was.' He clicked through a few more slides of Victorian studio portraits. More blanketed mums, more historic bubbas.

The library's collection contains hundreds of images like this: photos that show the now-redundant contortions required to photograph babies before you could just snap them as they crawled about the room, bounced in a Jolly Jumper or lay on a sheepskin rug. In all these photos the mothers become clumsy ghosts. They lean back out of the shot, lurk behind curtains or hide under blankets. A woman's face might be concealed under a big hat as she reaches, improbably far, to steady her child.

The German artist Linda Fregni Nagler famously collected—and, in doing so, rendered visible—this sub-genre of early photography. Thanks to her, these images are now known as 'hidden mother' photographs and her artwork of the same name, *The Hidden Mother*, was shown at the 2013 Venice Biennale. It's a collection of these portraits, approximately one thousand, exhibited together.

The art historian Geoffrey Batchen writes that Fregni Nagler's work reveals 'unspoken, even unspeakable, anxieties and commitments' around parenthood. Studio photography was expensive and laborious in the nineteenth century, so getting a portrait taken suggests a very deliberate act—much more intentional than snapping a photo on your phone. Batchen asks,

> what is the function of a portrait of a young boy or girl, as yet without identifiable physical features or personality and lacking any distinction other than the triumph of having reached childhood? A portrait of such a child affirms before all else the fertility of its parents but is also a sign of those parents' anxiety, at the possibility of loss, first of the child, and then of a memory of that child.

Despite the clumsiness of their characteristic gesture, in hidden-mother photographs the 'presence of a cloth-covered parent behind the child therefore signalled at least one important thing to any viewer: this child is still alive'.

Contemplating these images in the dark, I was struck by how little we knew about these women and their babies, not least because they are usually catalogued with titles like 'Unidentified Woman and Child' or 'Morgan Wife and Baby'. As with all archival documents taken out from under beds and given to public institutions, 'the displacement of [these] photographs from the individual to the collective . . . has certain consequences. The original viewer, an intimate of the subject (probably the very parent hiding in the picture), has been replaced by us, no more than curious strangers.'

To me, Batchen's academic tone muffles the emotion he wants to illuminate—why not just say that even historic parents love their babies with painful intensity?—but I do agree with him. Me, Mark, the class of sleepy students: we were just a roomful of polite visitors to these nineteenth-century lives, theoretically interested in what the photos 'mean' and the abstract ideas inherent in laying them side by side, but also preoccupied with fighting off naps, thinking about lunch and holding hands with our crush.

Sometimes it's different at work. Sometimes, when I look at other people's photographs I get the sense of something unbearably tender, as if the images cannot hold everything they've borne witness to since being taken. In those moments meaning rises from them like vapour. What would these portraits have meant to the people whose lives they momentarily interrupted? What would this photo have conjured for the hidden mother later, as her life expanded beyond the photographer's frame? The warm weight of the baby in her hands. Her sore and heavy breasts. The baby's small gurgles and fluffy hair. A damp photography studio. After the photo, did she bundle up her child, pay the photographer and walk back home? In my mind, I let her amble slowly, talking quietly to her small charge. Maybe she hurried, restless to return home to her other children and hundreds of chores.

And then, the sense of my own intrusion bubbles over. I need to leave mother and baby to their day. In the dim auditorium, I won't let myself wonder how long each baby lived.

*

As a little kid I was so mesmerised by the story of my own birth that I instigated an annual ritual the night before my birthday. *Vicky*, I would always ask, *what were you doing on this night six—or seven or eight or however many—years ago?*

My mother, perched on the side of my bed, would oblige as she tucked the duvet around me. *We went to KFC for dinner that night,* she would say. *You know, the one down on Kent Terrace, all of us—me, your dad and the big boys. And then—my waters broke in the toilet!* (Here, she would leave the dramatic pause she knew I loved, only taking up the story again once she'd handed me my favourite cuddly toy.) *When we got home, I couldn't sleep so I stayed up reading my book,* Cold Comfort Farm. *Your big brother woke up at 3am, and I made us Milos. At five, your dad drove me down to the hospital in Newtown. Belinda from next door came over to watch the three boys.* Then Vicky would smile at me, lean down and kiss my forehead. *When we turned onto Helen Street,* she'd conclude, *the sun rose at the bottom of the hill like a giant fried egg. I was so relieved when I met you.*

After her story, I could then snuggle down surrounded by

a small army of stuffed animals and concrete facts, a script I now knew almost by heart. KFC was on Kent Terrace; Henry and Vicky drank Milo when they couldn't sleep; the sun rose at the bottom of the hill.

As an adult I can sense the other facts that hover behind Vicky's story. My older sister, Charlotte, died of sudden infant death syndrome (SIDS), better known as cot death, just after Christmas in 1983, almost exactly four years before I was born. One birthday my mother said to me, of the morning I arrived under the fried-egg sun, *You looked nothing like your sister had. There was something reassuring about your stocky wee body, like you'd stay put in the world.*

I was not my mother's first daughter, but I was now her only daughter.

*

Here is everything I know about my sister.

My mother had two daughters, who both smelled like calamine.

Charlotte was the only person for whom objects and rooms were named in our family's loud, cluttered house, which meant someone happened to speak her two syllables almost daily. Vicky had given everything in our house a fun name. I didn't realise until I was twelve, for instance, that InSinkErators weren't called 'Gurdy Guzzlers'. 'The Snug' was the shabby end of our large airy kitchen where my dad kept his computing equipment and medical textbooks. But Charlotte was the only human namesake.

'Charlotte's Tray' was a flat basket, painted white with a blue ribbon plaited through the sides. It sat at eye height in the kitchen cupboard, holding our family's domestic medical supplies like Band-Aids, Panadol, the thermometer. In the summers after we came home from swimming in the Ruamāhunga river my mother would always ferret out the calamine for our bug bites from Charlotte's Tray.

My mother had two daughters: one tethered to her desk, the other eyeing Disraeli cautiously.

'Charlotte's Desk' delineated the border between the Snug— my father's domain, where we had to be careful not to bump anything—and the rest of the room, where we could shout and jump as much as we liked. Vicky kept her nicest writing paper in the top drawer of the desk and displayed her favourite trinkets on top. Stone mouse, metal jug, amphora vase of fabric flowers, marble bust of Disraeli. She'd rearrange flowers while she talked to her friends, cordless phone cradled between her shoulder and ear. My mother sat at the desk to write thank-you cards to everyone who sent flowers or casseroles after Charlotte died. No one explained who Disraeli was, so I assumed he was another absent relative. My grandfather perhaps, who had also died before I was born.

Once there were two little girls: one carried from the room in her mother's speechless arms; the other sneaking in, spooked by an imagined unnatural stillness.

'Charlotte's Room' was a sunroom off my parents' bedroom at the bottom of the house. My two oldest brothers, Henry and Rufus, had also slept in there as babies but after Charlotte died my mother refused to let her next two children, Humphrey and me, sleep there. It kept Charlotte's name, even though my father eventually took it over as his workshop and I only dashed in when I was desperate to steal solder or electrical tape from his toolkit.

Once there were two babies: the first a gift planned and longed-for, the second an accident.

When I thumbed through our copy of Janet and Allan Ahlberg's *Baby's Catalogue*, I always paused at the first page to stroke my grandmother's loopy handwriting in the corner. *For my dear Charlotte, with much love Grandma Dorothy, August 30, 1983.* Another pause: when I tucked my teddies into bed, safe underneath a colourful woollen blanket, I would rest my hand on their lumpy forms. My aunt had knitted the blanket for Charlotte when my mother was pregnant. These objects, only incidentally mine.

Sitting on the lawn one summer afternoon, I frowned into an undrunk Cup a Soup. Wellington harbour twinkled in the sunlight and I cast my mind over the question of who or what Charlotte was. She was a baby. I was seven. I must be older than her. But I had never met her.

The younger girl alone now, frowning in the sunshine on the lawn, asking *Who is older? Her or me?*

*

And then, as the years unfurl, how else does my sister arrive? When does she tap me on the shoulder or stroke my cheek unexpectedly?

At my sixteenth birthday party a beautiful blond boy from St Pat's ripped off a leg from Charlotte's Desk. I snatched it from him, furious. Murderer! The desk sagged and then collapsed while the music played into stunned silence. As if conjured, my mother walked through the front door to see me dissolve into tears, holding the amputated leg.

Charlotte, as if she had just stepped out of the room, amused.

(Ah, that poor beautiful boy. How was he to know? He came back a week later, escorted by *his* mother, to apologise.)

When I was nineteen, I was unhappy so I would swim two kilometres a day at the pool near my house. Once, as the new pool attendant handed me my change, I noticed her name badge read *Charlotte*.

'That's my sister's name,' I said, as if I used that word all the time.

'It's a great name,' said Charlotte, beaming and handing me my change.

My sister smells like chlorine.

At parties in my twenties I would meet people I didn't know very well. We'd laugh and make small talk late at night, leaning against the kitchen cupboards at someone's flat in Newtown. We might talk about our jobs or where we grew up. If we swapped facts about our families, people were often charmed to find out that I am the baby of my family, and that I have three older brothers.

'Wow,' they'd say, 'and no sisters?'

'Yeah . . . no sisters,' I'd say, the small unsaid fact nearly tripping off my tongue.

*

My sister is the tiny friction in an answer, the crunch of statement against reality. I don't have a sister but I'm not my mother's first daughter.

Once, in my late twenties, a counsellor asked me, *And how many children did your parents have?* I was hypnotised at how cleverly framed the question was, how the counsellor could do her fact-finding without assuming someone's parents had children only with each other, or that their family were all alive. *They had five.*

I went to see Laurie Anderson's documentary on death, *Heart of a Dog*, in the Film Festival, and afterwards, as my friend and I put on our coats in the Embassy foyer, I burst into tears. 'Stupid Laurie Anderson in her stupid spiritual movie said babies who die of cot death feel no pain and that they waft away gently from the world. Fuck her because she doesn't know and fuck her because she doesn't know what that does to people. You can't make cot death beautiful.'

My friend laid her hand on my back and waited for me to finish. 'I think the bitch stole that idea from Buddhism too,' she said gently.

Once, there were two women: one with a theory about death, the other sobbing in a lobby.

In my early thirties, another counsellor told me that SIDS deals the worst kind of 'what if' to grieving families. A baby has such a brief life and leaves so little behind her, only a few months of memories and no thoughts or opinions that relatives can cling to. Even well-meaning friends don't know how to connect their own memories to the absent child.

Without much to go on, the what-ifs start to swirl out and away from her, across the floor and out the door.

I try to imagine what Charlotte would've been like. Would she have been a Charlie or a Lottie? In my head she looks a bit like me, all dark eyebrows and round face and straight brown hair, but she's shorter, with our mother's narrow hips, whereas I got the softer, rounded frame from my father's family. I want to make her funnier than me too—a little more cutting perhaps. Decisive where I falter, intrepid where I am all nerves, *she* would have moved to London at twenty-two. I dress her in NOM*d. She'd overcome a wild youth to be the kindest of women, adored by her partner. I wonder if she would've wanted children.

Of course, this Charlotte is just a composite of all the Cool Older Girls I knew growing up, the girls I admired and later wanted to emulate. For years, I scrutinised other people's sisters, searching for evidence of mine.

Part of the challenge is that I don't have a place in my body for Charlotte. Not in the way I do for people or even animals who have died but that I got to love in real life.

After my cat Caspa died, I was bereft for weeks until I started seeing visions of her while I did yoga. She appeared during savasana, curled up asleep somewhere that felt like my soul, a warm grotto, dimly lit and cosy. This image came with the kind of realisation I might have in an all-too-vivid dream. *This is where she has always been.*

Driving home from a movie one night, Vicky glanced at me from the driver's seat.

'How are you feeling about Caspa, honey?'

'It's going okay, Ma,' I said.

'You must still be missing her at home though?'

'Yeah of course.' I paused. We rounded the corner into Adelaide Road. 'I keep seeing her everywhere y'know, like by the fridge, on the bed, but it's always just a crumpled tote bag or a jersey.'

I wanted to stop and apologise. It didn't seem fair to keep talking about a cat, because when my mother was the age I am now she lost her daughter.

*

A few months ago, I finally read the piece my mother wrote about Charlotte for the *New Zealand Pregnancy Book* in 1991, eight years after she died. I pulled the book off the shelf in the university library and sat down at one of the tables looking out over Wellington harbour. The only other person at my end of level 6 was a guy in a beanie and skater-fit chinos eating Subway and skimming his LAWS121 course reader.

It's a tiny essay, only three pages. Barely long enough, you'd think, to chart the trajectory of what happens after you find your baby dead one morning. *Horror brings disorder with it*, Vicky wrote, *and my memories from here on are vivid but confused. Grief and guilt descended with equal speed and equal force. Holding her waiting for the doctor, I heard someone shrieking her name aloud, and realised it was me.*

LAWS121 Guy balled up his Subway wrapper and threw it into the bin. He didn't look over at me. Speaking from inside her essay, my mother is exceptionally brave and unflinching.

> *I was grateful to everyone who tried to lift the burden of personal liability off me. All the same, I couldn't doubt that my smoking and trying to keep thin during the*

pregnancy, the dotty action-packed life Charlotte had led in the days leading up to her death, the cold bedroom, and the boys' streaming colds had all contributed to loosen her grip on life . . . In comparison [to the guilt], my grief over the loss, although overwhelming, felt very pure.

It doesn't say this in the essay, but after Charlotte died Vicky cried every day for six months, until my eldest brother, who was five at the time, asked her to stop crying because it was making him feel sad. After that, she made sure she cried at night after she'd tucked my brothers into bed.

I even became fond of the huge egg-shaped pain that ran along the inside of one arm, across my breasts, along my other arm, and then extended out in front of me, phantom-like, as though marking my embrace with a vast ghostly baby. Aches that I felt in the air in front of me didn't seem odd. Agony was the only bodily condition with which I felt comfortable. The rare times I felt briefly happy made me guilty anyway. How could I have forgotten my darling for two minutes?

After ten months of acute pain, my mother's burden began to lift slightly, as if someone had opened a window and a breeze drifted in.

My baby daughter was mine to cherish in my memory.

I looked up from the book. With a dull thump, like a balled-up Subway wrapper landing in the bin, I realised that I had forgotten the third woman in this story. My mother, who said my sister's name the most, and who knew the weight of both her baby daughters, heavy in her arms. I felt tears ooze down my face and plop onto the book. My whole

life, I'd only ever glanced at my mother's grief, as it swirled
and morphed above me.

My mother had two daughters: one dead and one alive,
looking up at her mother's grief like a murmur of starlings.

*

During a lockdown in 2020 I did all Vicky's shopping. One
Friday morning, as I planned my trip to New World, she
texted me her list as usual: Bread spinach fish peanut butter
earl grey tea. I let her know what time I was going and put
my mask in my pocket, fossicked about for car keys. My
phone pinged again: I forgot mayonnaise. Thank you darling.
Today is Charlotte's birthday. She is 38. I feel very sad. Usually
I cope much better.

I messaged my mother back: I thought about Charlotte this
morning too. Happy birthday Charlotte! 38 is so grown up. As
always, I wish I knew what she was like. I send you a cuddle
for today's sadness Ma. You have always been so brave about
her.

My mother had two daughters: one dead and one alive,
witnessing her mother's grief like mayonnaise.

My mother lives alone in south Wellington, in a small
wooden house where the wind slams at the windows and
the floorboards creak with a century's worth of footsteps.
Her kitchen is always light and warm though, and when
you stand at the sink you look out over her tiny back garden,
into three other tiny back gardens. As I pour a cup of tea or
scrub a pot other people's lives fall into my pocket. A cat
sits pert on the back fence. The magnolia drops a petal onto

the lawn. Someone squeals from a birthday party next door. If I haven't visited in a while, she sends me photos of her garden: a cloud of pink cherry blossom, electric alstroemeria, gargantuan echium.

Vicky has papered the kitchen walls with photographs of her children and grandchildren. It's her one-woman archive, her shrine, gathered from hundreds of emails and WhatsApp messages. We're all there, over and over again: me and my three brothers. We look sleepy one Christmas morning in the nineties. We gather at the beach with Grandma Dorothy. Henry's children perch in a pōhutukawa tree. Several people graduate. Humphrey's daughter waves a jammy hand. The whole family squints into the sun at my wedding. Humphrey (holding his son) stands next to Rufus (holding his son, who, in 2017, is missing two front teeth).

The photos climb up almost to the ceiling. They jostle for space and overlap one another with their curled edges. Most are crumpled from the steam that rises from Vicky's cooking. She always replaces a picture when the cheap printer ink fades from the sun. After I told her about reading her essay, she said, *Would you like to look at photos of Charlotte?*

We sit at her kitchen table with a heavy blue leather photo album in front of us. The sticker on the front says *1983*. It's just one of forty-nine family photo albums all stacked in the bottom of a wardrobe. Vicky used to say that she was a tourist in her own life, snap-happy every chance she got.

She opens the big blue cover. 'Lots of these aren't great photos, sorry, but we felt desperate to keep them all. When she died, this film was still in the camera.'

I look down at the photos of Charlotte, photographed the way babies in the eighties were always snapped, wriggling about in onesies, or naked in a plastic bathtub. I know from listening to Mark at work that these are called dye-coupler prints.

In one photo, my mother looks unfathomably young. Her dark hair hangs heavy to her shoulders and she stands with her back to the camera. She's holding Charlotte upright in her arms, and Charlotte looks directly at the camera over Vicky's shoulder, a small chubby hand aloft like she's about to wave. She has dark eyes and a soft fuzz of brown hair, a little ski jump nose. Vicky, in profile, gazes at her baby daughter, their heads so close together.

Now, I am crying again and some of my snot drips onto the album. 'Sorry,' I say, and wipe at the page with a tissue. 'Sometimes it feels so unfair, Ma.'

My mother looks at me and then down at the album. She turns the page. Charlotte lies on a sheepskin rug, beaming at the camera.

'You always remember how they felt,' she says, 'or their wee giggle. You know, Charlotte really did smile like that— like a tiny maniac.'

From my mother, I can learn a lot about my sister. Her life was short, only four months long, but very real: made of sensation and warmth. Safe arms. Soft kiss. A prickly woollen blanket on the floor in the morning sun. Milk. Her older brothers blowing raspberries to make her laugh. Her mother and father contemplating her with love, and stroking her face.

Charlotte arrived in the world the quickest of all my siblings. Vicky had two hours of contractions and then, all of a sudden, there was Charlotte, wide-eyed and in the world.

'She was the most serene of all you five, too,' Vicky said. 'She barely ever cried, everything just seemed to please her.'

I laughed. 'Not like me, huh? Didn't I refuse to walk?'

Vicky smiled. 'You were easy too. You all were, bless you, but Charlotte, she was something else.'

The altar of my mother's kitchen shrine is her fridge. The best photos are printed out A4 and stuck on the door with ceremony. Among these, five small baby photos sit in a neat row, right at eye height. They're all dye-coupler prints pulled from 1980s photo albums. Five gummy babies grinning back at the camera. We are lined up in age order: Henry, Rufus, Charlotte, Humphrey, Flora. When people ask about those photos, Vicky says *I have four children, but I had five babies.* She doesn't add that she still thinks of Charlotte every day.

Just before I leave her house, my mother and I hug at the front door. For a second, we are more than the sum of our two bodies. I feel Charlotte between us, not as a space where a grown woman's life should be or as a series of what-ifs, but as a presence binding us together in the doorway, a permanent weight in my centre.

The next morning, I turn facts over in my head, silently treading the path of sisterhood while I also walk to work. Charlotte and I will always have the same middle name, Victoria. As a baby I wore her hand-me-down jumpsuits so we've felt the same soft fabric against our skin. The first sound Charlotte and I both heard was the same woman's heartbeat, resounding through her body, one ordinary pulse at a time.

/

The Raw Material

Reduced to its essentials, weaving is an interlacement of two sets of threads at right angles to each other.
— The New Zealand Woolcraft Book

When I first learned to weave, I began with the two most common structures of cloth: plain and twill. Back then I didn't even know cloth had a structure, like plant cells and buildings, or that these structures had names. But it's true, there have always been words for how threads cooperate to form fabric. You see, weaving is a process of transformation, of two entities morphing into a fresh, surprising third. Warp, the lengthwise threads. Weft, the crosswise threads. And then, just like that: finished cloth.

In plain weave, warp and weft are evenly balanced. You just alternate one thread over another, again and again and again. Thanks to its simplicity, plain weave cloth boasts admirable qualities. It is very hard-wearing and reliable, quick to make but not prone to fraying. It has no right side and no wrong side. Plain weave hides nothing. Its uses are both sacred and domestic: flags and sailcloth; sheets and pyjamas.

In twill weave, one weft thread passes over multiple warp threads, which gives it a characteristic diagonal impression. This cloth is more durable and warmer than plain cloth, yet also softer and more pliable. It's slightly more sophisticated and less symmetrical, perhaps ever so slightly louche: it can drape and lounge around the body while also hiding stains. Wearing twill weave, you can look slinky and get grubby. This is why denim is woven in twill. Look down at your jeans. Do you notice those quiet diagonal lines rolling across your thigh? When I first started weaving, this is where I fell in love—when I was handed words that rendered something visible, something that seconds before had been anonymous but hiding in plain sight.

Early on, my weaving teacher, Christine, and I planned my first project sitting together at a café. She learned to weave in her late forties, after returning to Massey University and studying textile design. I was drawn to her healthy reverence for the unknown and her relationship with her tools. *Looms are like musical instruments*, she once said. *They have a mind of their own, so don't be disheartened when yours talks back to you.*

Christine had originally trained as a botanist and her scientific habits of attention meant she was also comfortable with the formulae and arithmetic of cloth. Every step of planning a weaving project is a mathematical exercise. It feels like geometry, excavating the right properties of straight lines (thread) to cultivate a plane (fabric).

I wanted to weave a blanket for a friend's new baby, so Christine made notes while my head swirled. Symbols covered her paper. Arrows here. Mathematical operators there. An important-seeming asymptote. Christine must have noticed my blank look because eventually she smiled and said, 'Don't worry if you haven't got this. It will all make sense when we're at your loom.'

I smiled back, pleased we'd unpick the formula again later, examine it at a snail's pace.

'You're not at work today?' she said, swigging the last of her coffee.

I shook my head. 'I'm taking a few days off. Doing less than I'm capable of. My boss suggested it.'

'That's great—more weaving time.'

What makes every weaver distinctive is how they approach their raw material. This is the wool and the cotton used to construct the cloth, but it's also more abstract than that. It extends beyond concrete substances because 'colors . . . words, tones, volume, space, motion—these constitute raw material' too, writes the Bauhaus weaver Anni Albers. A weaver's craft comprises the ways she draws from this well—how colours, words and volume preoccupy her mind. How do you plunge your eyes and hands into the world around you?

Some weavers plan meticulously, before taking a tape measure to triple-check the width of the loom. Their notes are neat. They make a plan and execute it. A loom is a computer and cloth unfolds from an algorithm. Other weavers seem to be more instinctive, somehow in tune with the qualities of their work in an offhand, celestial kind of way. They listen to their thread, touch and smell it. They do a rough sketch, then see how things go. Trial and error feature heavily. They lay their warp on the loom, eye it gently and take it off again. They might put several different weft threads in the one warp, not minding if it leaves the fabric lumpy.

The best weavers probably marry both impulses.

*

What I didn't tell Christine was that I'd been crying a lot at work recently. Tears gurgled out of me in the toilets and as I reshelved collections in the basement. I wheeled my trolley and my soggy face through the heavy automatic doors between one silent vault and the next. It was bad archival practice but while I was underground it felt safer to weep. I preferred it to crying in the loo as someone gathered toilet paper from a squeaky roll in the next cubicle. Something about where I ate lunch, the tiny garden behind St Paul's Cathedral, calmed me enough to do my job. I watched the pigeons potter about and threw them bits of my half-eaten sandwiches. At my desk, I pulled myself together enough to send emails.

Soon enough, I was blindsided by a colleague in the stairwell. He tapped me on the shoulder, and I jumped at his look of surprisingly earnest concern.

'Hey, is everything okay? I feel like you've been really quiet in meetings recently. You're kind of . . . pale?'

Despite myself, I was touched. Lewis was the only colleague who sent my work back to me requesting edits and I didn't think he liked me. I didn't want to answer him honestly but my body gave way and fat tears ran down my cheeks. 'No—nothing's okay but I don't want to talk about it.'

'That's fair,' he said gently, 'but let me know if there's anything I can do.'

I ducked past him and into the toilets.

To weave a blanket you need three things: warp, weft and a loom. You start away from the loom, though, constructing the warp. I built mine using a warping board, a heavy wooden frame with fat dowels sticking out of it. As you slowly wind thread after thread around the dowels, the board keeps them untangled and taut, mimicking the tension of the loom.

There are special tricks for winding good warp comfortably, so that it carries an even tension and your threads don't sag or bounce but spring back when firmly tapped. Wind with a steady yet relaxed arm. Your movements should be smooth, coming from the hip not the wrist. Plant your feet firmly on the floor. So much of weaving is like this: a practice poured from the vessel of your body, responsive not to language but to the mute demands of rhythm and touch, kinetic memory.

I spent an autumn evening winding bouts of wool in the spare room, while the wind rattled outside and rain spat at the window. Christine perched on the bed, thinking aloud and scrutinising my technique. I drew cream wool from a plump spool on the floor and guided it around the warping board. To keep the wool even, I murmured *over, under, over, over*—and back again—*under, under, over, under*. Winding warp felt like a balm, as though if I concentrated on the wool, kept my body gentle enough and my mind still, I'd make something perfect.

'Good girl, nice tension,' Christine said. 'Smooth movements. Don't forget to count.'

The smell of lanolin filled the room. I'd bought the wool, undyed, from a sheep station in the Wairarapa and occasionally I felt a tiny sliver of hay knotted in the wool's soft twists, as if I couldn't forget the paddock of fat sheep, nibbling grass.

As I wound warp, being systematic and deliberate, my breathing slowed. After I finished every bundle of warp, I tied it up—using the surprisingly and threateningly named 'choke ties'—eased it off the dowels and braided it into a plait.

The problem was that Pat had kissed someone who wasn't me. In a fit of suspicion one night I read his messages while he had a shower and the one that read I think we should talk about what happened on Saturday night lanced my chest. I careened through the bathroom door.

'What the fuck is going on?' I shouted into the damp room. 'You LIED.'

Pat flinched. I yanked open the shower and grabbed him by the arm. He lurched out, naked and dripping with water and soap. He glanced warily at me and then leaned over to turn off the shower. The room gawked in silence while he pulled a towel down, wrapped it around himself.

He exhaled. 'I'm so sorry. We kissed.' And then, 'Can I get dressed?'

'Fuck. You.' I strode out of the bathroom.

I can't remember how long we fought for after that, but I think it was hours. I think I shouted about truth and trust and boundaries. I dredged up the most venomous word I could muster: divorce. Pat pulled on his trackpants and sat on the floor against our closet. He rested his wet hair against the door, shut his eyes. I sat on the bed sobbing, ignoring his explanations and apologies. Humiliation washed through my body.

'You wouldn't have lied if you loved me,' I spat.

He looked on, at first merely stunned, but then comprehension mingled with shame, and a sad tide ebbed over his features.

The next morning Pat hardly met my eye as I flounced around the house. I banged my empty cereal bowl on the bench, sighed conspicuously as I combed my hair.

'I don't need a ride to work,' I announced, then paused. 'Actually, I don't think I can look at you,' I said, before marching out the door.

Luckily it didn't take me long, jangled and staring into

my computer screen at work, to regret the worst of my bombastic behaviour. Yes, something in our relationship had split, come unstuck and burst into a mess, but no, I didn't want to get divorced.

'I'm sorry for raising the spectre of a break-up,' I said to Pat after work.

He nodded and agreed, said he didn't want to get divorced either. We left it at that for now. An uneasy truce.

The main purpose of a loom is to hold the warp neat and taut while you pass the weft from one side of the cloth to the other. One afternoon, Christine and I crouched down beside my loom, our heads level with the warp as we eyeballed how evenly it flowed across the wooden machine.

'This is looking really good,' she said, standing up and walking around to give the warp a firm pat. 'Springs back nicely.'

Mine is a countermarch floor loom, which means it's big. Encased in its wooden frame it's nearly as tall as me and it sits, all two cubic metres of it, among the rest of our cheery mess. Pat uses it as a stake for a rubber plant and as a place to prop up some paintings. A lamp perches on top. My tall stack of weaving books teeters alongside it on the floor.

The practice of transferring your warp bundles to the loom, then threading and tugging them into the right position, is called 'dressing' or 'warping'. It can take a day or a whole week because the weaver will handle every single warp thread. My blanket, for example, had 672 warp threads. The dressing time had still surprised me though, because I expected all the energy to be in adding the weft, all those hours spent passing a shuttle backwards and forwards across the warp.

'Well,' Christine had said, 'the warp is literally half the cloth so of course it takes ages to prepare.'

Weavers call this kind of revelation 'loom time'. You just take the next step in the methodical process. Each phase will take as long as it takes.

Unlike winding warp, which generates a slow meditative rhythm, dressing the loom is a complex, erratic dance. The weaver walks all around her loom, first crouching and peering, now standing and tugging at bundles of thread, now pushing the rubber plant out of the way and winding the loom's ratchet in a wide smooth circle. *The New Zealand Woolcraft Book* describes the most visceral moment: 'Stand at the front of the loom, grasp the warp at the first choke tie and give it a good shake and a pull, or even slap it briskly.' A brisk slap? It sounds absurd but it corrects any disturbance to the length and tension.

There are moments when the dance slows right down, mainly during the last three steps, each of which reads like a slice of small poem: 'threading the heddles', 'sleying the reed', 'knotting to the apron-rod'. I spent the evenings of a whole week leaning into the middle of my loom like a mechanic under the bonnet of a car, hooking each warp thread through the correct heddle and reed slot—which are the devices that raise and lower threads, and control warp spacing.

Dressing is complete when the whole warp is knotted to the front of the loom, wound safely onto the back, and pulled taut between them. Eventually, I stood there, running my hands backwards and forwards across the warp's complete width. You can't tell by looking if you've tied it to the correct tension—it's a knack only your hands can develop. I have to shut my eyes when I pat the warp because sight confuses my instinct.

Albers calls this form of knowledge 'tactile sensibility'. She observes how we've lost the habit of relating to the world in this way, despite its primal importance. 'We have grown increasingly insensitive in our perception by touch, the tactile sense,' she writes. 'We touch things to assure ourselves of reality. We touch the objects of our love. We touch the things we form.' Albers understood that a weaver is always navigating a tension between sight and touch, words and movement. Sometimes, only our hands can tell us the truth.

At home, while we waited for an appointment with a couples counsellor, Pat and I were practically silent. We offered each other cups of tea and watched the same TV show at night but we walked on tip-toe, staying as quiet and still as possible. All the crying at work left me composed enough at home, but rage pierced my skull when I least expected it. If I glanced at Pat, idly scrolling his phone on the couch, a voice wailed in my head: *How. Could. You.* I responded by banging pots in the sink when I did the dishes. I willed him, through a clenched jaw, to look over and ask me what was wrong. He didn't ask me, but only because we both knew exactly what was wrong. He also seemed further away than I could have ever imagined, preoccupied and deep in thought.

The next week, while we were both at work, Pat emailed me to say he'd figured something out. Knowledge had dropped into his lap like a stone. His behaviour was the painful, spiky end of a problem with drugs and alcohol. He'd decided to stop drinking and stop taking drugs. He wanted to start again, and to start our relationship again, without substance abuse. I gaped at the email, aware of a ringing in my ears, and then, uncharitably, I rolled my eyes. *How convenient.*

A few hours later though, after sharing my sandwich with the pigeons and avoiding Lewis lest he ask another kind question, I opened Pat's email again. I reread his hundredth apology and felt something akin to truth ping like sonar in my stomach. Almost involuntarily, another voice said, *Well, that's quite a brave thing to admit.*

If you can't picture me sitting at my loom, just imagine me at a piano. The keys, waiting expectantly underneath my fingers, are the warp. My bare feet rest on the peddles, and my back is straight, but relaxed. I press my foot down and the heddles rise, bringing with them 336 threads, exactly half of the warp. With a small flick of my wrist the shuttle glides through the open warp, unspooling its cargo of weft thread. I catch it with my other hand and reach for the beater which pulls the weft into place, snug inside the warp. This movement is no more and no less than closing the lid on a piano. Then I take my foot off the treadle, and the warp is smooth again. I repeat these steps hundreds, if not thousands, of times.

Albers, as always, is right. As soon as I sit at my loom it's very clear that my hands know more than my voice does. When I weave, I discard language, stashing it in the basket where I keep my scissors and a darning needle. All words dissolve from me with a small sigh and my hands become soft from the lanolin in the wool.

Our counsellor was called Lorraine. In her first email she recommended a book describing the practices of 'emotions-focused therapy' for Pat and me to read together. I bought *Hold Me Tight: Seven Conversations for a Lifetime of Love*, blushing, at Unity Books. I hovered in the craft section first, pretending to check if there were any recent weaving books I'd missed (there weren't), and waited until Self Help was empty before scuttling over. All the staff on the shop floor were ten years younger than me and had glowing skin. No one with a septum piercing would be in a relationship that needed a book to help sort things out. When a young man, warmth radiating off him like a tropical holiday, asked if I needed any help, I shook my head.

'I feel so old, and like . . . shrivelled, Lorraine,' I said in our first session a few days later, draping myself over the side of the couch in her office.

Lorraine laughed. 'Flora, I see people in their *seventies*. Believe me, you two are getting a head start.'

Pat and I sat on opposite sides of the couch, not touching or looking at each other. We addressed Lorraine rather than our partner.

As my first blanket took shape, on all those days off from work, the repetition of passing the weft came to feel like a devotional act. I thought about my friend's baby and the blanket I was constructing for her. I tried to understand it in the terms I was learning from Albers. 'Material surface, together with material structure, are the main components of a work,' she wrote. My blanket's material surface, the image or pattern I could see outwardly, was a twill weave called 'Finnish Bird's Eye'. Flowing across the plane of cloth with a lilting or drifting quality, it looked like waves. I knew the blanket would gently drape and protect my friend's daughter from the cold.

The material structure, those elusive qualities emanating from inside the blanket, felt more complex. It was developing qualities of pliability, sponginess, and I felt it couldn't help but absorb traces of my thoughts about the baby. Each pass of weft was a single, tiny impulse towards love. From the outside, this part of weaving looks boring but, really, the rhythm leaves you in a trance; it offers up a kind of incantation. I was reminded that from the moment our ancestors started making cloth, they used it to make a kind of magic. People would infuse their intentions into the garments that wrapped their loved ones. You could weave a protective red hem there or a bountiful yellow flower there.

As the blanket started to grow, though, I could tell it was going to be a wonky artefact with wobbly edges and a bumpy surface. I had to remind myself of Christine's stance, her acceptance of the spirit that inhabits all looms. *You know, I'm realising that my big loom doesn't like too much humidity*, she'd said one day. Over time, all you can do is observe the machine's habits, its quirks, and learn to trust it. I made peace with the fact that my loom had decided to give the blanket a different purpose than I'd intended. I guess this will need to be an outdoor blanket, I thought. My friend could tuck it around her daughter in the pushchair or lie it out on the grass. From there, she could gaze at the sky.

Lorraine's main method, it seemed, was to reinterpret my and Pat's statements back to each other in the most generous way possible. When one of us lobbed an accusation across the couch she'd pause and say something like, *What I'm hearing is that you really need your honey right now*. She asked us gently probing questions about our early experiences of affection and what our parents' relationships modelled to us. How did we think we needed to behave to be worthy of love? Lorraine and *Hold Me Tight* taught us a new vocabulary: protest behaviour, attachment style, love language, denial.

When one of us baulked at how much work it would take to overcome seven years of avoiding conflict, Lorraine just smiled. 'Oh, you two are going to be absolutely fine,' she said, waving her hand. 'It's obvious how much you respect each other.'

Pat was seeing a counsellor alone, too, and thinking hard about his relationship with drink and drugs, but he was still quieter than usual at home. I'd glance over and see him staring through his book or pausing while he did the dishes, his hands in the sink. I'd resolved to try very hard to leave space for the silences, since a) I guessed it took a lot of brain time to examine how addiction had slowly burrowed into his centre over two decades, and b) I'd recently accused him of being shut down.

'I'm not, I dunno, *articulate* like you, okay?' he had said, throwing up his hands in our second session with Lorraine. 'I need time to think without you giving me your hot takes all the time.'

'But I don't know what you're feeling when you're quiet,' I said. I didn't feel articulate. I couldn't explain that his silences sent me the same blank message, no matter what he was feeling, be it despair, anger, exhaustion, boredom or a hangover.

Pat stopped. 'Oh. Fuck. You're right. You can't read my mind.'

I sighed. 'No. *You're* right. I need to let you figure things out for yourself.'

We both sat silent then, mutually chastised. Lorraine looked at us affectionately.

At home, her influence had started to bubble up too. Honest conversations just started to appear, as if they'd always been there and we'd simply overlooked them, like glasses on the coffee table. Perhaps we were already a little braver.

'I didn't come right after Europe,' Pat piped up suddenly one night, holding a sudsy plate. It took me a minute to follow but then I got it. Years of slow-burning reliance had burst into flame six months earlier when we spent six weeks in Europe. We succumbed to lavish habits. We visited museums, slept in, got proper tans, drank wine every night and partied as much as we could handle. After our six-week bender culminated in a five-day mega-bender, Pat hadn't been able to return to normal.

'God, do you remember that dealer guy, Ivan?' he said. 'I was terrified I'd have to go meet him, my palms were sweating.' He shuddered.

For me, our whole trip took on portentous, nightmarish hues.

In trying to capture the weaver's habits of awareness and attention, Albers argues that their 'acceptance of limitations, as a framework rather than a hindrance, is always proof of a productive mind'. I think for her, weaving wasn't a method to reduce the world to a simple binary, but a way to interrogate it. The weaver's idiom, as Albers calls it, refers not just to vocabulary but also to viewing the world in terms of structure, how different objects interact, and the resulting harmony. Weavers observe everywhere the counterplay of forming forces: 'the sea slowly grinding an evenly walled piece of glass . . . into a multiform body suitable for adoption into its own orbit.' It's nearly impossible to see in real time, but through the slow repeated rhythm of the ocean, even sharp glass transforms and softens. It takes on the qualities of the ocean and becomes one with it. What at first seems

chaotic is the just pulse of the universe rearranging itself—
you only have to pay enough attention.

I first noticed the shape of my own mind changing when
I could understand, with blinding clarity, the meaning
inherent in a tea towel. After dinner one night I said I'd
do the dishes—I was calm enough now not to bang the
pots about—and became distracted by the tea towel in my
hand. They are often made from waffle weave, a complex
and spongy structure that takes after its namesake. In the
kitchen, I could suddenly interpret what it had to say, how
it advertised its own function. The recessed warp threads
increased absorbency, but floating weft threads allowed the
fabric to dry quickly.

'Okay, now I need you to say that to *Pat*, Flora, not me,' said
Lorraine firmly one afternoon. And then as an afterthought,
she smiled. 'With eye contact too, please.'

I looked at her, pleading. She just nodded. I inched my
head around to look at Pat. It felt like it took minutes. 'Patrick.
Hi,' I said. 'It, um, scares me how much I need you.'

Pat gave a watery nod but didn't look away.

For at least the first five years of our relationship I
wouldn't admit that I needed Pat. I'd say instead *I want you
a lot but I don't need you. If we broke up, we'd both be fine.*
Well now. Isn't it funny when you realise you've been lying?
With one brisk flick of his wrist, Pat had accidentally ripped
off a Band-Aid and shown me just how much I needed him.

'Are you okay?' he said in the lift on the way down to the
car.

I nodded. 'You?'

He nodded. After the weekly hour of counselling, we
were always unsure of how to step back into the real world,

the world of picking up something for dinner and replying to texts from friends. Seeing Lorraine left us tender, even polite and careful, around each other. As if we were stepping over a flood plain, carefully picking up sticks from flood debris. We didn't know who would make the first move to touch again. Usually, it was Pat. *Oi, c'mere*, he'd say and bundle me up in his arms. At the end of a long day, I'd breathe into his work uniform, catch the scent of dirt and grass he brought with him. I may have had to give away complacent assumptions about my marriage but at least my husband still smelled like dirt and grass.

Maybe it's a fool's errand to summarise addiction because it's complex and looks different for everyone, but what I learned from Pat in Lorraine's office is that for years he'd needed to cultivate a numbness, a buffer between him and the world. Eventually, that buffer crystallised into a glacier that became its own burden. He was buried under it, and no one could reach him or dig him out.

'It was just so many things, all day, every day,' he said. 'Like waking up ashamed every Sunday because I couldn't remember the conversations I'd had the night before. I'd see someone the next weekend and start sweating, not knowing if I was repeating myself but knowing *they* knew.' He looked at me. 'I'd have to get drunk to be able to talk to anyone at all. Then it all starts again.'

My heart scrabbled inside my ribs as it all tumbled out, all these things I'd never known about him. There were many stories like this, which added up to a big gluggy tarpit of shame. Not just blank spaces where memory should be, but whole weeks of the Sunday blues, our clumsy stilted fights, regretted comments, his brain never not coiled around the next something to drink or smoke, or the consequences of drinking or smoking. Unlike me, who felt blindsided by his email, he'd borne witness to his own slide into isolation. Kissing someone else was just the thousandth cut, a desperate way to find connection when he had none.

'It makes sense that you kissed someone else, Pat,' I said, trying out the words before realising their rightness. He'd been completely alone.

'Can you say that again while touching Pat?' Lorraine asked. She wanted us to graduate from eye contact to holding hands. So, I placed my hand in his and felt the warmth emanating from his palm. Like most couples, we have always held hands the same way, fingers intertwined in the same pattern, over, under, over, under.

We were driving down our street in the rain when forgiveness landed in my body. Water bucketed down and the windscreen wipers squealed across the glass. We were quiet, tied up in our own thoughts, on the way home from therapy.

SQQUUUEAAAAK, said the windscreen wipers. We both winced.

And then Pat said, 'I know how much I hurt you, and I hate it.'

SQQUUUEAAAAK.

'I can barely stand it,' he said.

I turned to look at him while he concentrated mournfully on the road. The clockwork that had been wound up for weeks between my ribs gave out with an exhale. Or maybe something settled in my chest like a cat in the sun, turning round and round until it nestled down. Its ease spread through my body.

I laid my hand on his knee. 'You know I forgive you, right? That it's okay?'

Pat glanced at me. He looked so tired. 'Are . . . are you sure?'

I realised I was. 'Yes.' I didn't know how to say the next bit though. 'I think . . . I think we needed something that big to happen, to jolt us. You were the only one brave enough to admit it.' Under my fingers, I could tell that his work trousers were a twill cotton canvas. I liked that my hands knew the answers to questions that three months ago I wouldn't have thought to ask.

At our next session we told Lorraine about the drive home. Her face fell, but then broke into a wide grin. 'Oh, I wish I'd been there! I always miss the best stuff.' She paused, eyeballing us. 'But there's still lots of good work left to do, mind. This is just the beginning.'

Looking back, Lorraine was never more correct: we'd sit on that couch for over a year.

One Saturday night, a month or two later, I stood in my friend Katie's kitchen, sipping a cup of tea while she got ready for a party. A glass-blower from Adelaide, a woman maybe fifteen years older than us, was staying in the front room after visiting Whanganui for a week-long glass conference.

After Sylvia let herself into the house and said hello, she switched on the jug. I think she intended to read her book, but the two of us just stayed in the kitchen, chatting and asking questions of each other. At my request, she narrated the whole glass-blowing conference, and after she learned I was an archivist, we analysed her personal archiving practice. I mentioned that I had been weaving for a few months.

'So, how did you get into it?' she asked.

'I did the Artist's Way,' I confessed, blushing slightly, 'and then at like, week six a new thought just appeared—I want a loom. I think I'd finally accepted I'm just the kind of woman who has soft, repetitive interests, if that makes sense? I like knitting and watching my cat.'

'Nice resolve,' said Sylvia. Something *thunk*ed in the dishwasher. 'So you haven't always wanted to do it?'

'No. But I guess I've always loved textiles, like clothes.' Sylvia nodded, sipped her tea. I kept talking. 'First I started sewing cos I wanted to know how clothes worked. And then I was like . . . wait . . . but how is *fabric* made?'

Sylvia thought for a second. 'That's really cool,' she finally said. 'It sounds like there's a deconstructive impulse to your art. You need to know the mechanics of things. Next you'll move to the country, get some llamas, start spinning wool.'

I laughed. 'I do feel like weaving is something I can study forever and never fully master, that there's always something new to know.'

You might think that Pat and I would find easy harmony once we were in counselling, but now small fights burst into flame regularly, as if we needed to do seven years of bickering all at once.

'Is this normal?' I asked Lorraine.

'Very,' she said. 'You've realised your old methods of communicating don't work, but you're still figuring out your new methods.'

At counselling, I would watch Pat talk and pay attention to the slightest shifts of his tone, how he placed his hands or eyes. I'd realised that it all actually mattered—every habit added up to the sum of our marriage. It was a practice we performed together, comprising our daily habits and gestures, executed with varying degrees of awareness and intention, moment to moment: not only the weight of his arms when he cuddled me in the night (comforting) or how we said 'I love you' (as a farewell), but how I sounded when I angled for a fight (really mean) or how Pat looked at me when we moved furniture together (withering).

'It's not my fault I have no spatial awareness,' I bleated at Lorraine. 'I wish he'd be nicer to me and not criticise. All I did was ding the gate with the drawers.'

'You expect me to be nice to you all the time,' Pat replied. 'Besides, it was only a *look*. I didn't even say anything. Can't we just give each other the benefit of the doubt sometimes?'

As I mustered my rebuttal, Lorraine turned towards me. 'I wonder if you have quite rigid ideas about perfection, Flora? For both you and Pat.'

I must have looked confused so she explained further. 'You interpret his look as criticism, but perhaps he was just finding the whole situation challenging? Maybe you were doing just fine?'

'Maybe,' I mumbled.

'She was!' said Pat.

Lorraine continued, 'And perhaps you do struggle when Pat shows emotions that aren't "positive"?'

Pat nodded. 'Sometimes I get frustrated now. Or sad. Or whatever. Before I was preoccupied with getting wasted, or actually wasted. Now, I'm lots of things. And maybe I need room to sort that out.'

'I hadn't thought about that,' I said, suddenly a little ashamed.

'I think what you two are exploring here is that you're both human. And isn't that just so beautiful?' Lorraine said.

Despite myself, I smiled. I'd always assumed my marriage

was harmonious, but maybe that was actually just silence. Now we needed to learn the harmony of daily honesty.

Our friends were curious about Pat's lifestyle change, especially when they saw him drinking kombucha at parties. Still much the same as before, leaning against the bench in someone's kitchen, chatting and laughing—just now swigging from a mug of cold herbal tea. *Did you know he had a problem?* people usually asked me. I hated this question. *No,* I wanted to say. *Yes,* I wanted to say. Did I know? Not really, but only because I'd been wilfully ignorant for years. It was easy, too, because everyone partied hard and Pat seemed merry when he was high and drunk, and never got mean. He was good at his job and had lots of friends.

How much was he drinking? they would also ask, a little uneasily. Everyone asked Pat this too, before immediately divulging how much they did or didn't drink, if they did or didn't take lots of drugs.

'It's like people want me to reassure them that they're not addicts too,' he said on the way home one night as we walked through town, 'but I don't know about anyone else. I'm still figuring myself out.'

Even I'd been surprised at how simple it seemed for him to just . . . not drink. He didn't reminisce about beer or talk wistfully about being high. 'I mean, I definitely don't feel dynamic or particularly interesting at parties anymore,' he said, 'but that's nothing compared to how grossed out by alcohol I feel now. Like, physically sick.' He made a face, before adding, 'I guess that makes me lucky.'

'Yeah, revulsion will get you a long way,' I agreed.

'Exactly. It's way harder to deal with all the reasons I drank in the first place.'

I patted him on the arm, sympathetic but not sure how to respond. I'd never understand what it was like for him, having taken the lid off his emotions in one fell swoop, newly sober at parties and now informal Addiction Education Officer to our friends.

In conversations he didn't want to quantify his habits, knowing that the gnarled kernel of his problem wasn't how much or how often, but the quality of his intention: he only ever got high or drunk in the spirit of oblivion. Most of the time he didn't even manage to get there, at least not on weeknights, because he still liked to go to bed when I did and wrap around me while I fell asleep. But completely severing from reality was never not the purpose.

One drizzly cold afternoon Pat went for a bike ride. Now that he never had hangovers, he could spend his Saturdays whizzing about the city, exorcising his energy, being buffeted by the wind. He would come home, cheeks pink and grinning, showing his beautiful wonky teeth. I was stunned to realise that the countenance he'd had since I met him, his sallow and solemn resting face, wasn't permanent after all.

I'd been weaving my blanket all day and my vision was starting to go fuzzy, the Finnish Bird's Eye pattern like an actual sea about to flow off the plane of cloth and onto the floor. I stretched in my seat, laid the shuttle of weft down, and decided to go for a run.

I jogged down towards Island Bay, expecting the footpath to feel like concrete underneath my shoes, to look at the hills and see suburbs. Instead, the road, the hillside and houses all unfurled before me like a bolt of heavy cloth.

I found out much later that this is a known phenomenon, the tendency of a weaver's practice to spill outwards from her cloth and into her life. The weaver Hannah Ryggen referred to this as *luftvev* or 'air weaving'. She would map out designs with whatever her eyes landed on: power lines as weft, trees lining a river for warp. Colours arose from the 'rubies and relics' she saw in museums.

Pounding along the Parade, I saw the seawall like a hem against the ocean. The ice flowers and rocks lining the shore resolved into the motifs of a rippling twill.

I explained this to Pat when I got home. 'Ah,' he said, 'it sounds like you've got weaving eyes now.'

To look at the world through weaving eyes, I realised, is to nearly reduce understanding to texture, repetition and colour, but also to feel everything from the inside out. It is to become hyper-aware of the qualities that allow me to make and remake—to drape, fold and ply any object. The natural world is a mutable reality, defined first and foremost by its softness.

The intensity of this experience, of how I could see the world if I looked properly, verged on spooky. No one had warned me that, without even trying, the weaver's idiom would enter my body and change my perspective so thoroughly. Luckily, I grew accustomed to *luftvev* and after a while I enjoyed whatever happened when I brought my weaver's attention to my surroundings. I can be soft too, I thought one day, when I caught sight of my armpit hair in the bathroom mirror.

I found it hard to explain to other people how our marriage had shifted. It was like examining a photo album and noticing someone standing in every single shot, someone you'd never noticed before, a ghost. Now that I had words and concepts, I couldn't unsee addiction and the way it defined our marriage. I used to imagine it as unrelenting drama, as something self-evident because it's out of the ordinary. Car crashes, job losses, theft, violence. This is still many people's experience, but what struck me was how the opposite of this horror was also real for me and Pat. The chaotic effects of substance abuse were stitched so tightly to our everyday interactions they were barely visible. They could coexist happily alongside the lovely parts of our life, like talking about books, the Saturday veggie market, afternoon sex and breakfast.

For years, Pat was constantly losing things: his wallet, keys, phone, eftpos cards. He seldom texted me back. When we first started going out I shrugged it off—at twenty-four lots of dudes were unreliable—but it began to gnaw at me when he moved into an apartment I could never get into, because a comical number of things had to be neglected for this to be the case. The intercom was broken. Pat never had a phone and, when he did, no data. Though I nagged him, he never got me a key cut. So, if I went to see him I'd sit on the stairs outside for half an hour until I could scurry in behind a neighbour or I'd just wander around Cuba Mall until Pat's flatmate checked his phone. I felt foggy about it, low-key humiliated and certain this meant he didn't like me all that much, but still unsure if it was a big deal or a small deal. When we fought about it he swore he loved me, but he still didn't get me a key. Eventually, I just moved in with him. I made jokes about learned helplessness and boys being useless. Point being, if addiction is actually death by a thousand cuts, there is always something else you can blame for each baffling cut.

Since he's been sober, Pat's never lost his wallet or his keys. He's a very reliable texter. **On my way home now honey, love you xx** he will message at the end of the day. What I had assumed was a maddening, surface-level personality trait was something else: someone preoccupied about the next drink or last night's blankness, slowly losing his brain's bandwidth to shame. Maybe all this is why I'd been able to stay ignorant for so long, why something this enormous could glide, unnamed, through our relationship. Or maybe I was oblivious because Pat spent those years turning the worst of his destructive behaviour inwards. Who knows.

Pat's always been able to see things I couldn't, anyway. It was only after a few years together, listening to him describe plants and walking with him around the city, that swathes of anonymous green developed texture for me. Specific flowers and trees grew names, became distinct from one another. Muehlenbeckia. Coprosma. Dwarf conifer.

In Europe Pat had stood, speechless with admiration, in the garden of a famous Dutch landscape designer. I ambled about on the lawn, feeling hot and sticky. I could see Pat walking from flower bed to flower bed, slowly, incredulous, mouthing *wow* and rubbing his face.

'What? What is it?' I asked.

'It's just . . . what she's done here. It's mind-blowing. The plants she's chosen for the shade spots are incredible. I would never have guessed you could do that but now that I see it, she's so *right*.'

I looked at a plot of small flowers waving in the Dutch breeze. I still couldn't see it. I just didn't know enough about gardening and hadn't known how to pay the right kind of attention in Europe. Pat had gardening eyes long before I had weaving eyes.

And then, one ordinary evening, I finished the blanket. All those woven hours came to an end after dinner. Huh,

I thought, just like that—a Wednesday. I put down my shuttle.

'Honey, I think . . . I'm done?' I said to Pat, who was reading his book, stretched out on the couch.

'Oh wow,' he said, unfolding himself and coming to stand at my shoulder. 'What happens next?'

'I wash it, I guess. I think that's my last step.'

Pat leaned over and stroked the plane of cloth. 'This is so lovely.'

I was almost right. I did need to wash the blanket but the first last step was to release the loom ratchet with a clunk and watch the fabric sag and relax. I snipped every thread that knotted it to the front beam, and then I unspooled it. Chopped threads fell to the floor.

Unspooling finished fabric is a surprising finale after so many weeks of a slow, meditative rhythm. It happens quickly, with one smooth tug that feels counter to the weaver's usual gentle, considered gestures—close to a party trick where you whip the tablecloth from a laden table. But every process needs its outlandish peaks, I guess, and that evening, the blanket rolled off the loom and into my arms.

I filled the laundry sink with warm water and the softest of baby soaps before I plunged the blanket in. Once, twice I submerged it in the suds.

'The cat's trying to eat the wool scraps,' Pat called from the living room. 'I'm gonna sweep them up, k?'

'Oh man, thank you,' I replied, up to my elbows in the sink, now rinsing the blanket in cold water. He was always so kind about my mess.

Afterwards, I laid the blanket out in the living room to dry, and exhaled. Only now would the threads lose their last vestige of loom tension and ease into their final shape. As washed fabric dries, all the tiny spaces between once-taut threads disappear and a blanket truly becomes itself. Here, the weaving process is complete.

It's also true that this was not even an end at all, but a beginning. The blanket would now live a whole life away from the loom. It would be scrunched and chewed and flapped about by my friend's baby, and find itself stained by grass or Marmite. It would be chucked onto the couch and thrown into the washing machine and washed time and time again. It may get holey and then—hopefully—mended.

What is it, I wonder, that makes someone finally capable of understanding their own difficult dark side? Is it just time? I'm not exactly sure when I became ready but it was months after Pat began to slow—and then stop—his half of our trickiest dances. I didn't even notice the incremental way all our conversations had worked on me—until suddenly I could behave differently. Like: one morning I finally learned how to fight fair, to stop lobbing hurtful names every time I was in pain, because sober Pat took way less of my trash talk.

'I would never ever speak to you like that,' he said. 'I'm sick of it, okay?'

I was stunned into silence. 'Sorry,' I muttered eventually. 'And yeah, you . . . always fight way more respectfully than me.'

'Thanks,' he said, and smiled. 'I know.'

Halfway through our next fight—an erratic debate about how long my showers were in the morning—I paused mid-threat and raised a hand. 'Wait, wait, wait. Sorry. I do want to keep driving to work with you. I think this is a protest behaviour.'

Soon, too, I realised I'd been protesting in different ways for years, like a confused toddler who can't use her words. On weeknights, I'd often sulk when I noticed Pat getting high or having another beer but I'd knot my anger to something tangential—undone dishes or a misunderstanding from a few days earlier. *You weren't reassuring enough about my bad day at work*, I'd hiss, while he looked confused, spliff between his fingers, hurt by the accusation because, in truth, he listened so patiently while I ranted about work. The fights I'd pick seemed unrelated to one another, and never about his quiet nightly disappearance from our shared reality. This, I think, was the first method I found for putting distance into our relationship.

And it was in this quiet, daily way that the distance between us grew until it sprouted buds and blossomed into an unlikely, awful tree. I would match Pat's absence with my own. I cultivated a rich fantasy life, the crux of which seemed to be reinventing myself in Europe. Every day at work I looked up jobs in London, and imagined moving overseas alone.

I also nursed an intense crush on a barista by my work. He was someone I didn't know but who was good-looking enough for me to project all my unmet needs onto when he handed me a long black. I laughed at his jokes and even borrowed a book from him once. I didn't tell Pat for months, instead feeding the sugary crush, focusing on it as the source of my restlessness.

'I think you should tell Pat,' said Katie one day, hesitantly. 'You're hiding things from him.'

But I didn't listen. I wanted to keep distracting myself from the pedestrian challenges of being married, all that horse-trading about cooking nights and TV shows. I think

I also wanted to give my and Pat's problems a headwater I could name: marriage was hard because I had a crush on someone else. But with this kind of reverse engineering, I only ever generated more problems, adding to the list of unsaid sentences, heaping potting mix under the tree. Pat took more drugs; I imagined telling the coffee guy I liked him. When I eventually took Katie's advice and confessed to Pat just before we went to Europe, I watched him curl inwards, impaled by my words.

'How long have you been feeling like this,' he said, eyes shut, grimacing.

'A few months.'

'I *asked* you if there was a vibe when you borrowed a book from that guy. So you lied?'

My mouth went dry. 'I guess I did.'

In that moment, I tried not to think about the number of times I had said to Pat *I don't need you. We'd both be fine if we broke up.*

This is all just to say, there are a million ways two people can turn away from each other.

When the baby blanket was washed and dried, all wrapped up in tissue paper and given to my friend, I made a mental note to ring Christine. I needed her help planning my next project, a full-size blanket in three-colour tartan: fat stripes of cream and chocolate brown, intercut with slices of navy blue. It was a weekend afternoon and my mind felt calm, preoccupied with the concerns of warp and weft. Pat was playing football at the park. I had my coloured pencils out, and an old maths exercise book, so I could sketch my blanket on graph paper. My calculations covered a whole page, too. Arrows here. Mathematical operators there. I glanced over at my empty loom, excited about the next project. These days it felt like a contemplation machine, drawing thoughts and emotions from my body, and I thought about all the strange days it had seen me through. It had been months since I'd hauled Pat from the shower, since he'd first emailed me to say he had a problem with drugs and alcohol. *How convenient for him,* I'd thought at the time. Remembering my own dismal prejudice, I cringed. And then, a new voice muttered in my ear, quiet as anything: *How convenient for you, you mean.* Something stalled in me. I placed the pencil down.

'I need to tell you something,' I said to Pat when he got home, football under his arm. I'd been sitting on the couch for an hour, too fidgety to keep drawing.

'Always, my honey,' he said, flopping down next to me and pecking me on the cheek. I wasn't sure I could look at him.

'I, um, think I benefitted from your relationship with drugs,' I muttered, before realising I had to be clear, direct. 'I needed you to be like that. It worked for me. Like, almost the whole time.'

As soon as I started to speak, my thoughts all leapt to the surface like fish. Oh, the repulsive clarity of it all. It suited me to be married to someone who cultivated numbness, who sucked up all his emotions, despite the cost to his own well-being, because I got to feel good about myself at his expense. While Pat always lost things, I played the role of grown-up, the one who kept our eftpos cards safe and who paid the bills, responsible like a Head Girl.

Pat was generous enough to laugh at that. 'That's very easy to forgive.'

'You're very sweet,' I said. 'But there's more.'

'I'm listening.'

I found the next bit harder to explain. 'If I didn't need to think about your emotional landscape, I could take up more room. I could have more reactions and bigger feelings. Like, do you remember when your nana died?'

When Pat's grandmother died, I had bawled at the funeral, snotty and hysterical, even though I barely knew her. Pat had rubbed my back, dry-eyed.

Sitting on the couch, I was mortified at the shelf space I had engulfed in our shared emotional cupboard, until Pat pointed out that he got something out of this arrangement too.

'I clearly needed the catharsis of *someone* experiencing emotion.'

This is where the effects of addiction on our relationship were most raw but also the most diffuse, refracted through so many layers of our behaviour they were all but impossible to see. It's something we will always be unlearning.

For years we passed a glob of emotion backwards and forwards between us, muddled about who was responsible for it. Because I had absorbed all Pat's emotions too, I grew especially jumbled, often certain that my feelings were caused by him. If you can't imagine this, picture me tired after work and with a tantrum brewing. About what? Anything really. I might, for example, be convinced Pat expected me to make dinner, even though he'd just offered to cook. What I interpreted as Pat's expectation was actually just my own guilt about not wanting to cook.

Like so much in every long-term relationship, it doesn't sound like much—just the stuff of faceless Tuesday nights. But the years are full of faceless Tuesday nights and each friction-filled moment added up and pasted our relationship until it was sticky with confusion. It was almost impossible to talk about anything serious, too, when we didn't know whose emotions were whose. It took me a long time to understand that all of this, everything that seemed so far away from parties and drugs, was all part of the pattern.

'I'm so sorry,' I said to Pat, my hands hanging between my knees. 'I . . . I've hurt you so much. I did so many things that made our life much harder than it needed to be. And I feel like I've barely taken responsibility.'

'Hey—hey, it's okay.' He placed his hand on my back. 'Look at me, love. We'll get there.'

It had been a slow, warm afternoon that was turning into a slow, warm evening. I finally looked at him.

'Okay,' I said, a bit wobbly, 'thank you. For listening. . . and for staying married to me.'

'Thank you for staying married to *me*,' he said.

After dinner, as Pat and I lounged on the couch, he laid his head in my lap, as he always did when he was tired, and with my thumb I slowly traced his eyebrows, and the bridge of his exquisite, crooked nose. My hands knew the distance from his cheekbone to his brow infinitely well. He shut his eyes and we were both quiet.

He smelled like dirt and grass. My hands must have smelled like lanolin.

Wyrm Farm

The worm farm crouches under the washing line, squashed between the woodshed and the council wheelie bin. It's a simple object: a big, black, plastic tub with four legs. The lid fits snug over the top, held down by a brick.

She bought it from Bunnings after noticing the larger-than-life worm smiling on the packaging. After half an hour in the aisles, searching for low-energy lightbulbs as her heart rate increased, the worm had piqued her interest. She stopped mid-step and jingled her car keys. Under its backwards cap the worm was jaunty. The thudding in her chest slowed. The worm had big human eyes. It looked plump, relaxed, casual—the kind of worm who didn't fuss about saving electricity at a tatty, damp flat, or the heat lost through draughts.

She wrapped her arms around the big plastic bin and carried it to the counter.

After that, whenever she hung out her washing, she had to shuffle around the worm farm to avoid the bucket of worm 'tea' at her feet. It wasn't a problem, just a new rhythm to the other chore. She would give the lid an affectionate pat because she was the flat's worm shepherd, mistress of the worms. The household food scraps, previously destined for landfill, now had elsewhere to go.

Her online vermiculture course was presented by a South African woman. In Margie's accent, caring for your *werms* was no more complex than composting. Keep them in plenty of food scraps, water and warmth. Let there be no onions. Crunch eggshells into edible shards for their calcium. 'This is my favourite part of the week,' Margie sparkled in *Part 1: Caring for your Worm Farm.* 'I'm feeding my werms their favourite wermy supplement.' On the screen she dusted her special mix of homemade powder over the week's vegetable scraps. Lime + cornflour + bran + LOVE was Margie's recipe.

In their home by the washing line, the tiger worms multiplied exponentially, getting chubby on steady meals of vegetable peel, leftovers, teabags and wet newspaper. In the negotiations, her flatmates had agreed to scrape their unfinished dinners into the ice-cream container on the kitchen bench—she and the worms would do the rest. Everything went into the worm bin: old sourdough starter, purple cabbage, broccoli stems, cold rice, carrot skins. *Worms like their food as mushy as possible*, Margie had said, so she chopped everything into tiny pieces. Worm food, she thought—mashing up brown bananas that never made it into cake—is the logical conclusion of a Dutch still life. She was still the only person in the house who sorted the recycling and remembered to take reusable shopping bags to the supermarket but now she had the worms. They were a team, a closed system. She liked following Margie's advice, too. One day she even bought a big bag of cornflour from Newtown New World and imagined the worms getting thick and rubbery on its glutinous power.

Worm tea is the wrong phrase, she thought one morning, untangling her sodden sheets from the machine. You would never drink a cup of it yourself. Spilling out from the tap on the tub's belly, the tea was silty like a river; nutritious, but not for humans—only for plants and soil. The worms had an ineffable skill. Everything they ate turned to sludge that was too rich, too good, for humans. The worms were not afraid of decay but revelled in it, were freed by it.

When she lifted the worm-farm lid she was mesmerised by the thick heaving mass of primordial life. By then, thousands of worms oozed through the colourful muck, some wriggling about alone, others tangled in pinkish-red clumps the size of a tennis ball. The clumps started slipping, dissolving, melting through some half-eaten sprouts as the worms slithered away from the sunlight, down into their muck.

She learned that, unlike the anthropomorphised worm on the packaging, worms didn't have eyes, hands, teeth or any of the features humans associate with eating. Despite this, her worms could munch through five litres of waste every week. She kept notes in her diary about what they liked best and what decomposed the fastest: brown avocado, mouldy pumpkin, yoghurt. A worm's gizzard, she read online, can be compared to a miniature suction pump. It coats food in saliva before it gets sucked down into the stomach. Eating this way, a tiger worm can chow through its own weight in food in a day.

How much would I need to eat in a day if I were a worm, she wondered, and then: how much would a worm need to eat if it grew to my size? At the supermarket she eyeballed the half pumpkins in a pile. I'd need to eat 120 in only 24 hours, she thought, before buying only three. The worm population was now eating more than her flat could provide from offcuts of human meals. So every Sunday she made a huge pot of pumpkin soup and let it go cold overnight, so it could develop a bit of a skin. On Monday morning she would pour the thick orange stew all over the worm farm. Worms flopped out every time she took off the lid. She gathered up the overflow with her hands and plopped them back into the farm, or in the bushes between her house and the neighbour's.

One weekend, she videoed the squirming clumps of worms on her phone. She watched them in bed at night when she couldn't sleep, when the day's racket was too loud in her brain or she'd watched too much news. She would let the worms lull her to sleep.

Recently she'd seen her biggest worm yet—though it wasn't one of her flock. Thirty centimetres long and thick as liquorice, it lay on the beach, dead. Her flatmate had nudged it with a shoe, grimaced and kept walking. But she had stopped and gazed down at the flaccid body covered in grit. She had picked it up, felt its heavy weight in her hands and dropped it in the bushes by the carpark.

Darwin's final book was about worms. She got it out from the public library and imagined Darwin as an old man, heaving himself out of bed to observe worms at their work, in his lab and in the woods near his house. People laughed at Darwin for paying such fastidious attention to bugs— but who had history vindicated? The Father of Evolution, that's who. Darwin cared about his worms' diet even more than Margie did. He tested their appetite on different kinds of leaves, took judicious notes. *Judging by their eagerness for certain kinds of food, they must enjoy the pleasures of eating,* he wrote. It was Darwin who first understood worms were responsible for aerating soil, for mixing it up so that fresh dirt rose to the surface. Worms, he explained, squirmed under every single centimetre of ground.

She looked out into the garden and imagined what it looked like under the lawn. How does the ground not jiggle? she thought. How is it so still? She imagined she could see the lawn shudder and writhe in slow waves on the backs of all those worms.

Then, in the middle of one night, she sat straight up in bed. Were small worms eating the big dead beach worm, turning its body into sludge? She imagined a wormless world and felt her heart race again. She calmed herself back to sleep by reciting worm facts she'd read on the internet. In an acre of land, the worm population will churn up roughly eight tonnes of soil in a year. Long ago, when worms, snakes, dragons and sea serpents shared the same spot in the human imagination, the word was spelled 'wyrm'. In linocuts and engravings, worms would stand on clawed legs, or they loomed over you with powerful tough bodies, the size of horses or houses.

She dreamed that night of her beach wyrm, alive. It was rehydrated and plump like the worm-farm cartoon, but it didn't have the backwards cap and it was the height of a horse. The wyrm's thick body flowed down her road in silky, muscled waves. It took its time—it didn't have eyes, of course—and turned its great blunt alien head this way and that to inspect everything it found: the neighbour's cat, trees, concrete, rubbish bags left out for the council.

At her flat, the wyrm slithered through the door, only just fitting. It bunted her body with its head, its damp and sticky mouth over her arm. The wyrm's warm saliva seeped through her clothes. She knew then that she was safe, that

she would be sucked into its gizzard with everything else—
the concrete and the cats and the rubbish.

They would all be turned to rich sludge and given back
to the soil.

Tapestry Lessons

In the carpark I noticed another woman wrestling a loom from her car. She was much taller than me and a lot older—someone's Amazonian nana—but otherwise we were each other's surprising mirror, both juggling looms while overflowing with elaborate armfuls. Car keys, handbag, bobbins, a tote spewing wool. The woman shut the car door with her hip and carried her loom towards the workshop, which was about to start, in a renovated barn alongside the motorway. Between the road and our barn, a high-ropes course entwined itself through dense pine forest, and all day the shrieks and triumphant shouts of high-octane team building would waft into 'Tapestry: Beyond Beginners!'

Few people would call tapestry weaving high-octane. It is the slowest of slow-burn activities, both repetitive and painstaking. Officially, the word 'tapestry' just describes a specific hand-weaving technique, one that creates a structure unlike anything found in clothes or blankets. Tapestry doesn't use mechanised looms, so it relies on the weaver herself performing every single tiny ritual. No shuttle to quickly unspool thread. No heddles to raise the warp. Instead, the weaver interlaces every single weft thread into every single warp thread with her fingers, over and under, again and again. Then (and this is the most important bit) she pushes her weft down until it covers the entire warp and the fabric becomes what's known as 'weft-faced'. Textiles woven like this are hardy, stiff and warm, intended to become soft furnishings—historically rugs or cushions to soften ancient rooms and stop ancient draughts.

Unofficially, what we consider 'tapestries' are those colossal medieval wall hangings you see in museums or in the background of *Bridgerton*. These superstar textiles are pictorial and often ten metres long, three metres high and weigh as much as me. They overflow with unhinged illustrations. Lords and ladies hunt unicorns. A king wrestles a plump cherub in a puddle. An immense ocean threatens to drown a castle. When I first saw a tapestry like this, I stood transfixed, mute. It loomed above me. The chaotic, peopled scenes seemed to radiate heat and noise, as if I'd stumbled into a vast gruesome party or otherworldly *Where's Wally?* I peered at the tapestry and leaned out to touch it, but a museum alarm beeped. I startled. I wanted to climb inside the artwork.

Inside the barn I waved to our teacher, Trish, and flopped down next to the woman from the carpark, dropping my tote bag on the floor. Wool rolled out under my chair.

'Hi,' I said, getting down to pick everything up. The woman didn't reply or meet my gaze. Instead, she seemed to want to fold herself under the trestle table. I asked her name and she replied like a tiny breeze, *Diana*. Under her grey bob, a smile darted across Diana's face and she began laying out tools in neat groups next to her loom: a bundle of bobbins to carry the wool, a wooden beater, a sharpie, a ruler.

When I first started tapestry weaving, I was struck by how ordinary and possible it felt, despite how wild the finished textiles always seemed to me. But it's true, for a loom I can use anything sturdy enough to hold the cotton warp upright and tight (an empty picture frame). I beat in my weft with whatever I have to hand (a fork, usually).

At the same time, tapestry weaving makes serious demands of my hands and my head, and has a mystical quality that carries me away. I can't ignore the impulse. When I weave my body becomes still and all my energy concentrates in my hands and their small, exact gestures. I stare at the plane of cloth, my nose only a few centimetres from my fingers as they pass the bundles of weft this way and that. I mouth numbers silently as I count threads. I have memorised the names and steps of a hundred specialist knots, too. Dovetail. Clove-hitch. After a few hours, my vision blurs and my fingers ache. My fingertips are tender from plucking the taut warp as if it were a harp. I finally sit back in my chair, happy and tired. Every time I weave, I pocket a new knot, and the joy that comes from learning tapestry unfurls as it does, softly over months rather than minutes.

At Beyond Beginners, I wasn't surprised to find seven women sitting around the table, and as we clamped our looms to the edges, we chatted politely and nodded overenthusiastically, grateful for small talk about traffic and whether we were allowed to use the kitchenette (we weren't). I was the youngest by probably twenty years. Everyone except me and a potter in her fifties seemed between sixty and seventy.

The most iconic tapestry weavers are Greek. In the *Odyssey*, the patient Ithacan queen Penelope is known for weaving herself out of marriage trouble when she was stuck at home, waiting for her husband Odysseus to return from Troy. She is the weaver we all want to be: hyper-talented and meticulous, an untouchable artist.

In another story, Arachne, a regular village girl, wove herself into trouble by joining a weaving competition with Athena, the Goddess of Handicrafts. They wove alongside each other for a day like some infernal Beyond Beginners course. Athena's work extolled the pristine majesty of the gods but Arachne, foolishly mired in earthly stuff like love and sex, wove a tapestry depicting the gods' romantic lives. The sensuous images enraged and offended Athena, who was also secretly jealous of Arachne's skill. *Hubris*, she snarled, before tearing the tapestry to shreds. As a permanent punishment she transformed Arachne into a spider. Humbled, Arachne could still weave but she'd be forever tangled in the web of her own life's making, honing her craft unseen in corners and behind shelves.

Tapestry reflects both of weaving's lineages, art and craft, in equal measure, but it is easily the kind of weaving that people are most likely to recognise as art. We can emphasise the features it shares with painting or sculpture, rather than with other woven objects, like blankets or tea towels. We usually judge a tapestry's formal qualities—the shape of its picture or its decorative capacity—not its drape or absorbency, how soft it feels to touch.

Medieval tapestries are clearly artwork. Their designs are rich and elaborate and ultra-complex, often copied from oil paintings. A single large tapestry would have taken a team of artisans months to weave. And accordingly—as befits art—tapestry making was seen as exclusively men's work for hundreds of years. They strode about busy, clanking workshops, and teams of apprentice weavers staffed huge looms taller than anything Penelope and Arachne would be strong enough to use. Each weaver had a skill to perfect: you were the weaver who wove hands or the one who wove eyes, maybe even the weaver who wove water or unicorn horns.

Making tea towels and blankets, meanwhile, has traditionally been women's work. At home, this kind of weaving kept most women's hands busy because every household relied on a never-ending stream of useful cloth: to swaddle the baby, to keep your husband in shirts, to shroud the dead. We don't know anything about these women who made fabric day in, day out, keeping warm by the hearth and chatting to one another, in bad moods or good, maybe distracted by new love, a sore cramping tummy or a growing baby.

The textile historian Elizabeth Wayland Barber suggests weaving became women's work because it blended easily with childcare. A woman's daily task needed to be repetitive enough so as not to take up too much of her attention. *Keep one eye on the baby at your feet.* It must be interruptible by small children. *Fetch the toddler some water.* And easily resumed once interrupted. *Where was I?* In this way, year after year, women drew fabric from the day's incidental moments.

Nowadays, of course, neither of these situations is particularly familiar. Cloth weaving isn't domestic labour and large-scale tapestry workshops no longer exist. Instead, almost all contemporary handweaving in Aotearoa is practised as a hobby. But women are still advised to tether it to their domestic space. *The New Zealand Woolcraft Book* asks you to consider 'where you are going to use the loom . . . A spare room, or perhaps a studio, sounds wonderful, but if the weaver is a woman, she will find that much more weaving is accomplished if the loom is in or near the kitchen.' Scornful, I clamped my loom to the kitchen table so I can talk to my husband while *he* cooks dinner.

My life—my kitchen—is less chaotic than most historic weavers'. I don't run a medieval household, and I don't have children yet. Sometimes my routines are so quiet that it feels like my life's texture could dissolve, float away in the wind, if I wasn't paying attention. Leave for work in the dark. Scrolling. Wait for the kettle to boil. Emails. My husband and I remind each other to ring our mums. One of us will text on their way home: anything from the supermarket, bub? We fold each other's washing.

After we'd set up, Trish handed everyone their 'cartoon'— the weaver's guiding sketch. Mounted behind your loom, it shows you what you intend to weave, reduced to its most basic constituent parts. A useful cartoon gives clear guidance but also leaves enough wiggle room for improvisation, for the weaving to take its own shape. Creating one is tricky, so Trish had drawn them for everyone.

Mine was derived from a picture of the sky I'd emailed her, a stock image of a sunset all decked out in lurid gold and pastel pinks, blues. Plump clouds that rivalled those surrounding Mount Olympus. Land peeked out along the bottom edge. I wanted to learn elaborate colour mixing, how to create naturalistic skies and landscapes, because so far my tapestries were extremely basic, limited to abstract scenes made from blocks, lines and circles. Sometimes I wove very stylised figures or words: a line drawing of a chicken, the phrase 'HOLY MOLY'. I am also a very slow weaver chasing flawless textiles, so I unravel anything that hasn't worked. I started the M in MOLY four times.

Next to me, Diana was planning to weave a beautiful woman's face. I marvelled at how Trish's cartoon showed her how to weave neck, mouth, nose, eyes, ponytail but also blushed cheekbones, contouring, a dewy forehead, the silky join of hair at the woman's nape.

Trish is the kind of person you're lucky to have in your corner. Smiley and warm—she's often wearing fluffy jumpers—she also exudes pragmatism and competence, like a good nurse or school principal. I suspect she's used to sorting out other people's mess (she'd brought only super-strength Bell for our morning cuppa). She also weaves like she's under a spell. Her hands fly faster than my brain can process and thread seems to unspool from her fingers and rove through the warp by itself. She is one of very few professional tapestry weavers in Aotearoa.

'Sorry,' she says to the group of us watching over her shoulder. 'I find it hard to weave slowly anymore. Let me do that again.'

Early in her career Trish collaborated with the artist Gordon Crook. He designed the image; she created the cartoon and wove it. At a recent exhibition of Crook's work in Page Gallery, I stumbled across two tapestries woven by Trish: *Rockpool* (1993) and *Cone* (1993). *Cone*'s single pert red seashell left me feeling gently silly, in touch with the world's most mundane yet lovely mysteries, like catching a stranger smiling at a text message. Something tiny, bright and lively burrowed into my chest. Maybe it was just delight at two unlikely worlds meeting. A wet, oceanic jewel rendered in soft, dry wool.

'I saw my work in Te Papa once,' Trish said, as she banged more weft into a loom across from me using short, strong taps. 'It was an exhibition of "Gordon's" tapestries. My son said, *Look mum there's your weaving.*' Trish handed back the beater. 'See how I've laid that, Sherelle?' She smiled, then stood up. 'My son was confused about why it didn't have my name on it.'

'Is that straight-up sexism?' I asked, unravelling some tangled wool.

Trish looked thoughtful. 'Well, some people think it's hard to know where the artistry lies. Is it the person who designs the tapestry or is it the weaver?'

I'd read enough to know Trish was right. Influential French tapestry theory argues that artistry lies solely in designing for tapestry, not in weaving one. An artist is someone who defines the vision, the workshop master. They have their intentions carefully recorded on the cartoon, like paint-by-numbers, and the weaver simply executes their wishes. A weaver must never interpret the cartoon using their own knowledge, lest it alter the artist's intent. Art has divine inspiration; craft a set of hands. To this day, all tapestry makers end up asking themselves the questions embedded here: *Am I an artist or am I a weaver? Or do I reject this distinction?*

Gordon Crook, who did technically know how to weave, considered himself a hybrid figure, an artist–weaver. But art historians note that he still insisted on the 'difference between tapestry weaving as an art form, the work of the artist–weaver, and the craft of tapestry weaving, in which the dictates of an artist–designer were rigidly followed'. Weaver–weavers still came second in Crook's mind.

I was very ready to villainise Crook, to imagine him pacing around the studio shouting orders, but Trish was generous. Despite his emphasis on hierarchy, he'd helped her develop artistically.

'Gordon was demanding, yes, but he challenged me to weave things I never thought I could. Intricate, fine designs; beautiful faces. I learned so much from his design process, too. When I saw what he did, how he created cartoons, I *knew* I had to design my own work.'

'What do you think Gordon learned from you, Trish?' I asked.

She laughed. 'I'm not sure. That I'll stand up for myself? That weavers need recognition?'

At Page Gallery, I was relieved to read *Weaver: Trish Armour* on the wall alongside *Cone* and *Rockpool*, to see her immense skill recognised and named.

Now, Trish designs her own cartoons, usually from collages of photography, drawings, paintings and prints. Her work, she has written, is preoccupied with both the 'weaving process and conveying human emotions and experiences in the face and form'. At the workshop, Trish explained that she felt most challenged and happiest weaving people's faces, exploring emotion as it exists in expressions. She is preoccupied with what weaving as a form, with its ancient connection to the body, can say about the body's experience. She also interrogates tapestry's long-standing relationship to architecture by reinterpreting the built environment back to itself through wool.

Visually, her tapestries retain a collage energy too: none seems quite located in a single scene. My eyes rove across Trish's tapestries and they feel like puzzles I want to solve. They expand towards contemplation and symbolism, almost iconography. Doves, swans and statues inhabit uncanny architectural spaces. A moth flutters across a contemporary imagining of a Greek myth. From one piece, a twenty-first-century Psyche gazes back at me.

Many weavers reject the distinction between artist and weaver on the grounds that to weave well you must master traditionally 'artistic' skills anyway: colour, composition and drawing. I agree but am not satisfied, because those skills remain secondary to the real core of weaving, interlacing one silky thread over another. I want *that* specific act valued for and by itself because I feel that's what lets me pose complex questions. When I weave, thoughts blossom, suggested by the movement itself. If I stare at the plane of cloth long enough, I feel something shift and move around me.

At the workshop, for example, as I scrutinised my half-finished sky inching slowly over the horizon of my loom, I decided that tapestry is deliberate and illusionary in equal measure. You work in a fundamentally binary medium with only two options—warp and weft. The threads overlap at single points, like coordinates or pixels, so nothing can be left to chance, and nothing can be altered once your weft is beaten. But it struck me then that the whole point of tapestry, despite the need for excruciating intention, is to disguise that idea; to hide the structure of the work; to make an argument for porousness; to let the weft wander; and to let colours flow and dissolve into one another.

It feels philosophically optimistic that I can build something so infinite from something so limited.

In the early afternoon, as everyone got into the rhythm of their work, our conversation drifted away from weaving techniques. I could only listen because I was concentrating so hard on my loom. With twelve different colours to mix, my progress felt painfully slow and my fingers clumsy.

'My daughter-in-law is pregnant, so I've just been doing all the grandchild knitting,' said Trish, peering at an error in someone's warp. Around me, the others nodded, as if to say *yes, the Grandchild Knitting*. Trish continued. 'Ah—you've just got this in the wrong place, Claire-Louise, unweave to there and you'll be right as rain. It's looking great.' She walked around the room. 'It's nice to have something so mindless to do with my hands after a whole day weaving. I just watch TV and zone out.' She flexed her right hand. 'I'm a bit achey, though.'

Diana nodded, now relaxed and distracted from shyness. 'I'm missing my grandchildren so much,' she said. 'My daughter-in-law is pregnant too, but they're in the UK. I've had to post all the knitting.'

I was impressed that Diana and Trish still found time to knit so much for their grandchildren. What did it take, I wondered, to make all these clothes and all these tapestries? I wanted to know how they became exceptionally good weavers while raising families. Did they tip-toe to their loom while their babies napped? When Trish's kids were little, she could weave only when they were at school, on the days she wasn't working. Now her kids are grown and she flouts *The New Zealand Woolcraft Book* by having a studio in the attic of her house.

When I said that Pat liked to buy wool with me, that he constantly encouraged me to spend our money on crafts, another woman was agog.

'My husband would never,' she yelped.

I blushed, suddenly feeling like I was bragging.

Talking to these women it struck me that my weaving and I were given another gift earlier this year too. Solitude. Suddenly, I was alone for six months when Pat spent a long summer working on an island off the coast of Whangārei.

With Pat away, I was living alone for the first time in my adult life. I would cook myself huge pots of vegetable soup, vats that would last a week, and weave at the table with all the windows open while it simmered. I cared for our ancient cat and talked to Pat on the phone in the evenings. The cat would sit in the open doorway with closed eyes, on the cusp of kitchen and street. She would raise her face to the air and sniff. Together, we passed the time quietly. My tapestries grew steadily bigger.

Penelope's weaving, practised while she waited at home for Odysseus, turned into high-stakes labour because she was inundated with suitors. They lounged about the palace and exploited Penelope's noblesse oblige and drank the cellar out of wine. They all wanted to marry her, but in the meantime they seduced the maids. To stall picking a new husband she announced she needed to finish her tapestry. *I'll marry again when it's finished*, she said. Penelope wove all day, a paragon of industry, but at night, lit by palace torches, she unpicked her work. She was the kind of woman who would re-weave the M in MOLY fifty-six times. In this way, Penelope fooled her suitors for three years, until Odysseus returned.

Penelope's craft is seen by classicists and literary theorists as evidence of her cunning. In the *Odyssey*, Homer even calls her 'wise Penelope' because she used her art, this canny cloth, to stage a protest. With tapestry, she could undermine the choices men kept trying to make on her behalf. It's a story that, unusually, glorifies a woman's craft abilities.

I find Arachne's story harder to interpret, and maybe even more interesting for it, because it ends the moment Athena shouts *hubris!* and transforms Arachne into a spider. It stops abruptly, like a mouth clamped shut. Sure, Arachne has been flamboyantly punished for her pride, but she remains a gifted weaver. I wish I knew what happened next or how Arachne felt in the following months and years, as she spun her silk and plied her craft, all while she maintained her web and caught flies. I wonder if the final act of this story, playing out in some corner far away from Penelope's palace, just celebrates a different mode of artistic production.

My weaving was not what I'd call high-stakes labour or a protest. It was just what flowed into the space Pat left, the thing that arrived when I submitted to instinct. I missed Pat a lot and was sometimes unnerved by the distance, but he was always caring and gracious, and eventually I felt okay being so far away from him.

As my hands worked too, in their daily trance, I began to feel not just calm but excited, full. After work I'd accidentally weave for hours in my yoga clothes, distracted by the loom on the way to getting changed. I left dirty washing in the basket for days, abandoned. I took up all the room in our tiny house, left bobbins on the couch and stacks of weaving books on the floor.

Now that I was weaving regularly—had snuck it into the endless cycle of ordinary days—my disdain for the *The New Zealand Woolcraft Book* dissolved. I started to find their advice realistic and weirdly encouraging. *Go on*, the book seemed to whisper, *start where you are. Weaving works with your real life and all your sticky obligations.* I now love to imagine women surrounded by thread in their kitchens, to think about everyone who's ever made art in a corner near the oven. They help me feel poetic on those weekday mornings when I find time to beat a few lines of weft before shovelling toast in my mouth and running for the bus. If weaving is art you create in a haphazard, domesticated way, then maybe haphazard, domesticated lives are art.

When Pat came home, he watched me weave with a resolute and affectionate scrutiny I found almost unnerving, like I was new to him all over again. When I gazed back, I couldn't help smiling. He stole a kiss. We were charmed by each other's novelty, the new open space between us. Why, he asked, did I put a ruler through the top of the warp? What do we call a single line of weft? He listened intently, before chopping basil and baby tomatoes.

In the late afternoon, the workshop filled with low winter sun and grew warm. Claire-Louise massaged her wrist, yawning. I glanced over at Diana's loom and saw a beautiful woman's face blossoming into life. Diana's hands moved quickly but deliberately. If Penelope was all guile, she was all tenderness.

My heart sank. I gazed at the clumsy work inching upwards on my own loom. I had to concede that weaving the sky was way beyond me. It looked nothing like the majestic heavens I'd imagined. Dumpy blobs for clouds, bad shading. The complexity of the sky—of all those colours, of following the outlines, of joining thread, of keeping everything even—had knocked me over. Hubris! Spider city, here I come, I thought.

'Don't worry,' said Trish, seeing my forlorn stare, 'Diana's been weaving for longer than I've known her. Also, I think you chose some . . . quite advanced shapes. Maybe we should focus on practising colour work or weaving the landscape. Let's leave the clouds for tomorrow?'

I nodded. 'For sure.'

She patted my shoulder and turned back to Sherelle, who was asking about something called soumak. In the silence, Diana paused and put down her bobbin.

'I'm only this good because I've been weaving forever,' she said, smiling properly at me. 'You've got your whole life to figure it out. Just keep going.'

I smiled back at her, lightness washing through me again. 'Thanks Diana, that's super wise.'

I turned back to my loom and picked up my bobbin.

At home, I knew I had dishes to wash, and I'd told Pat I'd make dinner.

But before I do that, I promised myself, I will sit down at my loom. I will abandon the sky and focus on the ground. When I finally get up, to stretch my aching fingers and boil some rice, invisible thread will still unspool from my hands, luminous.

Bogans of the Sky

'It's like the white noise of smells down there,' Tom said. 'It's everything all at once, every nice smell and every bad smell you've ever smelled.' He shook his head and picked at the couch. 'It's worst when it's just been raining, and then the sun comes out and warms everything up.'

I sipped my tea and nodded. I knew what he was talking about. For most of my life I've also lived within smelling distance of Wellington's Southern Landfill, and on certain still, pink evenings a thick, sticky aroma clings to my street and the surrounding hills. It wafts up from the tip face— that gully being steadily filled with waste—and it's not bad necessarily, just sickly sweet and dense. To me, it marks the edge of my city: a few minutes down the road from the tip a tiny pebbly beach called Ōwhiro Bay looks out over Te Moana-o-Raukawa and Wellington finally stops.

This smell is how you know you live near the tip face because the tip face itself is impossible to actually see, even once you're inside the Southern Landfill complex. It's nestled at the end of a deep valley, concealed around bends and spurs, away from the recycling centre and the scrubbed concrete bunker where we throw our rubbish. Only commercial users are allowed to drive their trucks directly onto it: building firms, landscapers, private waste companies, the city council itself. My friend Tom fits this bill. Every week he drives out there and stares straight into the raw centre of the landfill process. He can breathe it in on those wet, warm days.

A few years ago, Tom's work drop-off coincided with what he now calls 'Meat Day', a random afternoon when the tip face bulged with supermarket waste, plastic-wrapped mince and chicken.

'It was like the apocalypse,' Tom whispered. 'The birds, they blocked out the sun.'

Above Tom's truck, the usually serene seagulls turned feral. They dive-bombed towards the rubbish, screeching. They tore mince from one another's bills. On the ground, hundreds of gulls strutted about, dangling bits of half-eaten raw flesh.

'Usually seagulls look so beautiful and clean,' Tom said, 'but they were all covered in blood.'

'Do you . . . like seagulls?' I asked.

Tom sounded indignant. 'Of course,' he said. 'They're the bogans of the sky. And what are they doing, after all? Eating our trash and pooping it into something biodegradable? Sounds like a favour to me.' Tom always carries bread in his truck to feed the seagulls who live in the central city.

A caw interrupted us and we looked out the living room window at two birds skimming above my street. Seagulls live to twenty so I must have seen many of the same birds, year after year. All of us, observing one another's little lives along the same coast, near the same tip. My seagulls, my tip. At least two old bikes and god knows how much else of mine is buried at the Southern Landfill.

*

True bird people, I notice, don't say 'seagull' because all gulls are technically seabirds. They also know that 'seagull' is a catch-all bucket used to describe three very different native species. So they slice off 'sea' and say 'gull', or they use the birds' specific names. In English, we index animals by their physical attributes, so these gulls are all named for their beaks and backs: the black-backed gull, the red-billed gull and the black-billed gull. In Māori they're called karoro, tarāpunga and tarāpuka, names that whakapapa to each bird's home inside coastal ecology.

Karoro, the black-backed gull, was birthed from the union of Tangaroa and Papatūānuku, a child of unsettled sea and sturdy earth. He can, after all, drink fresh water or salt water as he chooses. Or he might be the son of Paraki and Hinehau, a long-winged glider using his wind-given birthright to travel kilometres out to sea on updrafts. His strong, long wings give him plenty of lift. Whoever his parents may be, Karoro's sisters, Torea and Te Ākau, will always keep him tethered to the shoreline. Up close, karoro's black wings and back, enveloping his big white body, can give the impression of a tuxedo. From a bus stop on Lambton Quay recently I watched a solo karoro patrol the awning of the CityLife apartments. The gull toddled among the air-conditioning units stuck on the side of the building. He puttered this way and that with the fastidious energy of a busy concierge. 'What are you up to, smarty feathers?' I muttered. But my bus arrived and I never found out. Whatever his ordinary bird business, it was opaque to me and my human eyes. Bird-book authors drop adjectives like sommeliers when then describe karoro. They are 'vigorous', 'bold and conspicuous', 'loud', 'persistent'. Karoro, they assert, are 'particularly abundant at landfills' and it's easy to imagine these birds strutting about the tip face on their bright yellow legs. But they haven't always been a nuisance: karoro were once kept with clipped wings as garden helpers. They pottered about nibbling slugs, keeping the kūmara plants pest-free. Useful, perhaps even pet-adjacent.

The other city gull is tarāpunga, the red-billed gull. Only about a third the size of karoro, tarāpunga are decked out in subtle silver–grey and white, except for their 'conspicuous red bill and legs'. Like karoro, tarāpunga are deemed an 'enthusiastic scavenger around rubbish dumps'. But unlike the pest karoro, tarāpunga are endangered. They seem like alert little birds, assembling in the empty park near my house as a southerly storm rages and water gathers across the grass in great puddles. These birds keep their own counsel. Only occasionally do they send an envoy to wheel and buffet in the pouring rain. When the sun comes out, the tarāpunga stamp their feet to make the worms think it's still raining and they keep snacking. They fly away when people return to the park. Kids boogie board across the puddles, now big enough to be considered small impromptu lakes.

The gull you won't see in Wellington is our third species: the little black-billed. She is known as both tarāpunga and tarāpuka, and I wonder if this is because she lives in the South Island, inside the Kāi Tahu dialect. Our other two species have names in many languages, but tarāpuka are endemic to Aotearoa and not known anywhere else. She is unique, like takahē and tuatara, and she faces 'an immediate high risk of extinction'—she is rarer than the rarest of kiwi. I have only seen tarāpuka once, minding her own business on Lake Rotoiti. She bobbed at a wary distance from some ducks and a family standing in the shallows, hurling slices of bread into the water. Eventually, the father seized one unlucky duck and tarāpuka drifted away. She'd seen enough.

You won't find any tarāpuka at the tip. It's just not their scene, a seabird expert told me recently. I mention her here simply to pay tribute to all three species.

The acting manager of waste operations at the Southern Landfill, Robert Hon, estimates their gull flock contains over five hundred karoro and tarāpunga.

'It's hard to know, though,' he adds, looking quizzical and leaning back in his chair. 'We can't really count them.'

Robert isn't flustered by this because, luckily, he's fascinated by the many problems landfill presents, both practically and philosophically. The exact number of gulls wheeling in the sky above the tip is just one more fickle variable.

'When you're doing earthworks you want to make any slopes as smooth as possible,' he says, 'and you want them to be as steep as possible. But there's a threshold, you see. At a certain point, a slope collapses.' He uses his hands to demonstrate the ideal pitch of a hillside, cleared and sculpted to give the tip face maximum space without it crumbling back on itself or tip staff. Robert trained as a civil engineer but almost brushes off his early career. 'Retaining walls, roads, bridges, all that stuff,' he says. 'You really only need a spirit level.'

Landfill, on the other hand, is a huge complex system, constantly grinding and spinning. Humans, machines, waste, wildlife, all tangled together. This complexity reflects the scale of the task. On behalf of Wellington, Robert and his staff are filling an entire gully—Carey's Gully—with rubbish, bag by bag, day by day. In a year they receive 100,000 tonnes of food scraps, building waste and green waste: sticks, branches, leaves, chairs, stained mattresses, glue, concrete, metal, mandarin peel, dog poo. They're building the tip face in a spiral formation that climbs upwards. It's the most mathematically efficient shape, Robert says.

It's food waste that lures the gulls. The flock flaps in around 10.30 every morning, when they know the trucks start to arrive, each one packed with the morning's kerbside rubbish collection. The gulls wait on the cliffs above the tip face while each truck raises its tray and gushes waste onto the ground. A bulldozer then flattens each load, driving this way and that for a few minutes. Only then does the flock dive forwards to gobble up the soft innards of each rubbish bag.

Robert observes the birds every day and admires their smarts. 'They've learned to wait until the rubbish is flattened, because food is actually only available after the bags are ripped by the bulldozers,' he says. 'We see them bringing juvenile birds, too. We wonder if they're teaching their young about the landfill.'

'God, so smart,' I said. 'They really know their way around the tip face.'

Unlike karoro and tarāpunga, the closest I've come to spotting the tip face is walking in the hills surrounding the landfill. Up there everything seems natural. The hebe grows densely, the taupata tall. It's quiet except for the *criiick criiick* of cicadas and your feet crunching on the dry, rocky track. You glance down and there it is, a slice of colourful, grotesque trash mountain snuggled in the very back of a valley; wilderness and wasteland mashed together.

'It was surreal, seeing something so gross from somewhere so beautiful,' I said to Robert.

He shook his head. 'It's really not a coincidence,' he said, before explaining that the hills around the tip experience a kind of 'DMZ effect'. By being so close to the landfill, the area repulsed the usual urban interests and, left alone by property developers, it flourished.

Every day, the tip flock flies off when the landfill closes at five, Robert told me. 'They lift off into the sky and we don't see where they go. Some south, most north I think.'

From where he lives Tom can also see the tip flock rise into the sky and flap away out of Carey's Gully. 'Where are they going, do we know?' he asked.

Tarāpunga are probably flying to their cliffside roosts further along Wellington's south coast or heading to a colony north of the city. Karoro fly to colonies by the airport, where they nest at Breaker Bay and Moa Point. Regardless of where they sleep, hundreds of gulls cross the city every day on the wind roads they've been flying for thousands of years. Wellington's gulls will have witnessed the land transform unrecognisably beneath them, bush ceding to lawn and rocks organised into buildings. What does the sky taste like up there now? I wonder. I imagine the old smell of damp soil, leaf mulch and salt erased by smoke, petrol and hot concrete, maybe a whiff of fresh Pantene Pro-V in the morning, rising from the public servants who school down Lambton Quay.

On my own walk to work one morning, I stopped and watched several tarāpunga paddling in the sunlit fountain at Te Aro Park. One bird took teeny gulps from the bubbling jets. Another submerged herself with a splash and popped up, preening with purpose. Others stood knee-deep and still, observing the activity around them like tired parents. The small flock seemed to be having a relaxed start to the day, unlike me, who was eating a piece of toast and listening to the news with wet hair.

Not so long ago tarāpunga would have waded in the many streams that flowed down into Te Whanganui-a-Tara: Kumutoto, Waitangi, Hape, all Te Ātiawa names you don't hear unless you go looking. The streams themselves were either drained dry or encased in concrete by the colonial authorities and now trickle under the city, hidden. Tarāpunga splash in the fountains built on top.

Standing there beside Te Aro Park, I wondered if these gulls registered the difference between river stone and fountain under their webbed feet. How did they understand the line that we Pākehā enforce, that hard boundary between the human world and natural world?

Long before the city discarded its dinner scraps at the Southern Landfill, it was a place for growing food, not rotting food. Te Ātiawa named the area Kaipakapaka and it was a large ngakinga, with good soil for potato crops. During a recent public talk, the Te Ātiawa historian Honiana Love gestured at the map of Wellington displayed behind her, pointing at a large area just over the hill from my house, between the city and the sea.

'Kaipakapaka was a garden out where the landfills are,' she said. 'The name, we understand, refers to the processing of fish. It's not far from the coast and it's not far from the kāinga that spread themselves along the south coast.' It was only one of many immense gardens in the area. 'They were working across the whole peninsula, right across over into Seatoun,' Honiana continued. 'These ngakinga didn't just produce food for one pā but for the whole region.'

After Honiana's talk, I tried to imagine Kaipakapaka as it once was, before it was alienated from Te Ātiawa. I see row upon row of potato plants in the sun and a solo karoro, who wanders through the leaves pecking at bugs. Nearby, people chat while they scale fish, placing each one to dry in the afternoon heat. I like to imagine someone threw karoro the odd fish tail. After all, he was doing the garden a favour.

A few weeks ago, I asked Graeme Taylor, a marine bird expert for the Department of Conservation, if gulls are considered smart animals.

'Of course,' he said. 'They're hunter-gatherers. And they've always fed on food that's not necessarily easy to find. I've seen them work in pairs to rip up a big fish carcass. They definitely display what some people call "avian cunning".'

I paused in my frantic notetaking to appreciate how Graeme's phrasing observed the small potential gap between 'bird' and 'how people interpret bird'. It was only what some people *call* avian cunning. He used the gentle habits of a long-time science communicator in our whole conversation. Ideas felt contingent; claim and counterclaim were calmly evaluated; moral categories were evaded at every turn. In Graeme's telling, gulls don't 'scavenge for trash' but rather, 'Some populations have learned to associate human behaviour with diverse food sources.' Their natural scavenging zones (beaches, shallow bays) have simply expanded inland (the tip, picnics, Cuba Mall). They've turned their formidable brains towards the richest food source possible: human waste. Graeme said he started studying seabirds because we knew so little about them, far less than about those forest birds. I decided that in a past life Graeme must have lived as a seabird himself, possibly an albatross.

Until I talked to Graeme I was amazed that 'at risk' tarāpunga lived as part of the tip flock—that an endangered bird lived off human waste. Surely not? Surely that was just some pigeon energy. It was like a kākāpō living in a public park, eating his way through a dropped bag of Twistees.

Graeme wasn't shocked, though, given how much he knew about tarāpunga. Their population has declined by fifteen thousand breeding pairs in the last sixty years. *Where do thirty thousand birds go?* I wanted to bleat. Tarāpunga's colonies have almost completely disappeared from their natural homes, all offshore islands. Now, when DOC staff arrive on an island expecting cliffs covered with chatty, busy birds they find the landscape empty and quiet.

'Tens of thousands of red-billed gulls lived on Burgess Island in the 1940s, and now . . . not a single bird,' Graeme said.

It's likely all these birds died because we overfished around tarāpunga's main food sources. Gulls can't dive deep into the water so they cooperate with other animals—like large fish—to corral krill at the surface. You can see it from the beach: a cloud of gulls circling the ocean, their unseen helpers just below the surface, snapping at krill's heels. But fish out the fish and the gulls can't feed. So hungry tarāpunga migrated to the mainland to feed on the one remaining reliable food source, our waste. This is a risky move because, onshore, tarāpunga become vulnerable to cats, dogs, cars and even karoro.

Telling me this, Graeme's voice raised ever so slightly. 'So, people think red-billed gulls are doing alright because you see them chasing after your chips, but what we're actually seeing is the last remnants of the population, scraping together a life on the mainland.'

'Christ almighty,' I said to Graeme, 'that's cooked. And people *still* don't like them?' Earlier that week I'd seen two tarāpunga pecking at a roti in Cuba Mall. Two teenage girls looked warily at the birds. *Ewww*, one had groaned.

Graeme looked thoughtful for a second and recomposed himself. 'Well, all gulls just seem very available to us,' he said. 'They're not a hard-to-spot wildlife. If anything they're . . . in your face.' He sounded almost sorry.

I should have asked him if he thought something like Bird of the Year could fix tarāpunga's branding problem and dissolve the complacency that attends their apparent ubiquity.

After our talk, I went back to work, distracted and kind of tearful. The whole afternoon I forgot to include attachments to emails and then I knocked over a stack of books. I was only wrenched from my sad reverie on the way home through town, when I nearly collided with a man wearing a Pikachu cap. He looked up from his phone, apologetic. 'That's a really stupid hat,' I growled to myself, surprised by the depth of my rage. On the bus home I wondered if this was how Graeme felt all the time, quietly grief-stricken yet surrounded by people who love only fictional animals. Poor Pikachu Hat Guy, though—for all I knew he had a tarāpunga cap at home.

In many ways, little red-legged tarāpunga has the familiar conservation tale. The twin perversions of colonisation and capitalism have eroded her habitat and now we owe her an urgent debt of care. But karoro, our big unruly bully gull, has written a much stranger story.

Thanks to trash, their population has blossomed—or exploded, depending on your perspective. In some areas, karoro are so unnaturally plentiful they actually threaten conservation ecology and get in DOC's way. As they flap back from landfill their droppings plop invasive seeds into nature reserves, and as effective 'aerial predators' they eat the chicks of much rarer birds, an unforgivably ruthless snack by human standards. The outsized population means that our relationship with karoro is defined by hostility or, at best, by what I'd call 'reluctant responsibility', which seems like a unique dynamic for native birds, when usually we give them names and breeding programmes. (It's true: every kākāpō and takahē has a name.)

Karoro are one of only two native bird species given no legal protection under the Wildlife Act 1953. Karoro (and the spur-winged plover) are currently excluded alongside a list of invasive pests, pets and the animals we eat. People can spend a year in prison for harming or even possessing any of the animals we know we need to treat like treasure if they're to survive, which includes tarāpunga and 393 other native birds, as well as 475 mammals, reptiles, amphibians and invertebrates. A decade ago, the borders of animalhood were even gerrymandered to give some insect species the necessary protection. Katipō spiders and giant wētā were 'hereby declared animals' for legal purposes.

Who knows if things will change? In July 2023, DOC announced that the Wild Life Act 1953 would be replaced, declaring it no longer fit for purpose. The press release even noted that 'not all native species are currently covered by the Act', though it didn't list which ones might be added. Even if karoro remain outside a new Wildlife Act, 'They are still protected by the Animal Welfare Act,' Graeme reminded me, 'so you can't torture them—but you can kill them. If birds are harassing flocks of sheep, putting sheep at risk, a farmer can shoot the gulls.'

As an organisation now inadvertently responsible for hundreds of karoro, the Southern Landfill has agreed to 'maintain' its flock, to monitor and manage them.

'Is this because the birds present a big health-and-safety risk to staff?' I asked Robert.

'Of course we're concerned about how birds impact the staff,' he said carefully, 'but let's put it this way—the guys out on the tip face are working with huge machinery and toxic waste. They have more important things to think about.' The Southern Landfill is the only local agency that accepts commercial construction waste. Concrete, plaster, metal rods, all mashed together.

'We also process the solid portion of Wellington's sewage,' Robert continued. He raised his eyebrows. 'Just think about that for a second.'

I scrawled myself a note: *staff are more concerned about asbestos poisoning and human faeces than getting pecked.*

The tip isn't managing gulls in isolation, either. Hundreds of pigeons, starlings and sparrows hop about the tip face too, cooing or chirping at staff. Every day, thousands of rats burrow into the rubbish, and in turn lure as many or more feral cats. The landfill's boutique food waste centre, which processes restaurant scraps, entices wild pigs from the hills. Wild goat and deer filter down too, grazing on rubbish. The place heaves with animals. A whole city farm ambles about the tip face, pushing their beaks and muzzles into ripped bags, sidestepping bulldozers on hooves or paws.

'Wow,' I said. 'Why does anyone go to Zealandia? Seeing animals is way cheaper at the tip.'

Robert nodded. 'Right? We've got some keen deer hunters on staff and we're always joking about this being a great place to hunt.' He paused for a second and let out a small sigh. 'No—we do bird work because seagulls fly into the flight path of planes.' Then he laughed. 'But, I mean, when you build an airport near the sea . . . you're gonna get seagulls.'

Ah, so here we have the rub. Karoro vs aeroplanes.

Apparently, the worst thing about karoro is that they are 'an extreme threat to aircraft'. The birds, wheeling around as normal, get sucked into plane engines and chewed up. The passengers might hear a *BANG!* A plane might have to make an unexpected landing.

In the airport's official report on bird strike, these gulls make the top of a long, thorough list of avian threats. They're colour-coded bright red, a shade mostly reserved for fire danger days or a serious national terror threat. In the report's identification photo, karoro stands on a rock piercing the choppy sea. He gazes back at the reader, yellow feet firmly planted, in a pose I choose to read as defiant.

The airport's wildlife officer, Jack Howarth, explained to me that karoro had been responsible for '60 to 70 percent of all bird-strike incidents at Wellington Airport' over the last five years. More specifically, the airport has proved that Southern Landfill karoro pose the highest risk of all. Three years ago, they commissioned a team of scientists—and a water cannon loaded with food colouring—to spray each of the region's tip flocks. Blue dye for the Silverstream tip, red for Kenepuru, orange for the Southern Landfill. Colourful karoro flapped around the city for weeks but it was almost exclusively orange gulls gliding across the flight corridor. The orange dye proved something the airport had long suspected. Karoro's commute to the Southern Landfill bisected the runway.

Now, airport staff work harder than ever to mitigate the threat. 'It's not about reacting to the birds,' Jack said. 'It's about predicting their behaviour and using that data to help us manage their impact. Airside crew report on the wildlife every single day.'

Binoculars and clipboard in hand, they document bird numbers, flight patterns and where they nest, feed and mate. Every piece of information is loaded into a database from which strong patterns emerge. Like, unusually large flocks of karoro seek out the tarmac under two specific conditions: for shelter during winter's southerly storms, and as it gets dark in the long summer twilights.

'The tarmac retains the heat and they're looking for somewhere warm to sit, like anyone,' explained Jack. 'Black-backed gulls don't have a set routine but we've learned their preferences inside out.'

Before talking to Jack, I'd wanted the airport to act as the villain in karoro's story, to frame them as the unfeeling, greedy defenders of planes against helpless birds—on the bird's turf, no less (the sky). But I was touched by just how much attention Jack and his team paid to karoro, how much they knew about karoro's life. Their scrutiny had qualities I associate with the practice of love, friendship and successful marriages: diligence, curiosity, admiration.

'People like to divide the world into "human spaces" and "animal spaces", but they completely overlap, everywhere, all the time,' Jack said. 'That's just how it is. And anyone who gets into this kind of work does it because they love animals—so at every single airport, non-lethal seagull management solutions are always preferable.'

Wow, I thought, what a mouthful. Non-lethal seagull management solutions.

The most passive strategies for dissuading smart karoro from the airport and Southern Landfill are diffuse and environmental. They rely on karoro associating the area with subtly hostile experiences rather than pleasant ones, like meeting an acquaintance who yet again doesn't remember you. Plant flax on nearby cliff faces: it becomes harder for karoro to roost comfortably. Plant special AVANEX grass around the runway: if karoro eats it, he experiences what experts call 'post-digestion feedback'. When iron-willed karoro inevitably perseveres through a tummy ache, raise the stakes. Employ less naturalistic strategies. Freak them out. Airside crew, observing too many birds napping on the tarmac, blast recordings of a gull's distress call from speakers on the main terminal roof ('audio-based disruption'). The gulls scatter into the air.

'But they're so incredibly smart, they tend to fly back five minutes later,' Jack said. 'They're habituated, they know how long the audio runs for.'

Years ago, at the Southern Landfill, they would fire a shotgun into the air, but karoro eventually learned to recognise and avoid the digger with the shotgun behind the seat. Now, the gulls are managed using a 'pyrotechnic solution': when the gulls seem too numerous, fireworks—loud and dazzling—are set off around the landfill. It seems to be effective.

'But again,' Robert said, 'we're relying on our best estimates here. We drive onto the tip and look up . . . sure, seems like fewer birds.' He shrugged.

Eventually, at the airport, the contest arrives at macabre theatre.

'Oh, we use seagull effigies too,' Jack said.

I looked up. 'Effigies?'

'Gull decoys that provide a visual warning. You place them in off-putting unnatural positions—one wing bent out of shape, that sort of thing. The pose depends on whether you want to replicate a wounded or dead gull.' Effigies are supposed to deter karoro by creating fear of local predators.

I looked up an effigy manufacturer's website and found it full of upbeat, badly capitalised advertising copy. They instruct us to *Use the Dead Gull decoy to keep seagulls away from landfills. Use the Dead SeaGull Effigy to Scare Gulls away from beach front homes.* To get the most out of their products, purchase two: *place one decoy face down and the other feet up.* Karoro, it seemed, was a wily opponent. You would have to keep the gulls guessing—move the decoy randomly every day or two. Duly noted.

Their karoro products looked meticulous and very finely observed. One product was a life-size decoy, dressed in that familiar black-and-white tux of real feathers, only this time hanging limply from its iconic yellow feet, modelled on *a dead gull in a death pose.* I wanted to know whose job it was to make these effigies. Did they research karoro photos online? Did they stand on a windy beach to observe the birds in flight, so they'd mould the wings just right? I imagined the artist standing back from their work, gazing at it, wondering if they'd placed the feathers correctly.

How sad, I thought as I shut my computer, that it's karoro's opponents who know him the best. Our relationship with karoro provokes a strange tension: in order to banish him, we have to know him extremely well. We spend all that time and energy, just to get rid of something.

Despite the focus on non-lethal management strategies, real karoro do have to get killed. Last year, the population near Moa Point had risen to eighty nests, above a threshold deemed safe for aviation. The colony had to be culled.

Jack was solemn. 'This isn't something people like doing.

The last cull before this was in 1993, 94.'

The humane way to kill karoro uses narcotics. You lace butter with a chemical solution called alphachloralose and slather it over slices of bread and leave them near nests; karoro eat the easy treat and pass out quickly. It's not the alphachloralose that kills them but heat loss. It's humane because karoro doesn't notice when he dies, and any 'non-target' species who have accidentally eaten the bread can be collected and revived, warmed up in incubators. Left outside overnight, karoro dies of exposure.

Robert said they'd only once tried to cull karoro at the Southern Landfill. 'In the nineties, we tried to poison the birds here too,' he said. 'But apparently the dosage was incorrect and some stayed awake long enough to fly away.'

There they were, hundreds of drugged up but not yet comatose karoro lifting off into the twilight.

'It wasn't long before they started falling from the sky,' he continued. 'Apparently one landed in the playground at Ōwhiro Bay School. It really upset the kids.'

I haven't found this story on the official record but, whatever the truth, the Southern Landfill never poisoned the gulls again.

When I spoke to Graeme the seabird expert about culling karoro, he seemed philosophical about its necessity within conservation, though he also added, 'They've been here much longer than us—they have every right to stay here.'

In the kitchenette at work one afternoon, a colleague suggested that we just can't get past the fact that gulls don't know how to share.

'You know when you're feeding them chippies at the beach,' she said, 'and they're screeching at you? And then

181

they start absolutely mauling each other over a chip? It's disgusting.'

I nodded. 'Yeah, they definitely violate our moral codes. They eat rubbish for god's sake. But also, that kind of impresses me,' I confessed. 'They'll do way better in the apocalypse than us.' I looked at her. 'I mean, did you know that seagulls can *drink* seawater? They have built-in desalination filters, these glands behind their eyes.' Drinking salt water kills humans, but excess salt just flows out a gull's nostrils, like mislaid tears.

My colleague paused. 'I respect that,' she said, before wandering off.

Putting my mug away, I was left feeling like I hadn't conveyed the true poetry of my point. Aotearoa is an archipelago and gulls, unlike us, are true archipelago dwellers, tethered to land, air and sea in equal measure.

At the end of our conversation, I asked Graeme if we knew how living off landfill affected karoro. Did we know how they were doing out there, aside from their growing enmity with planes?

He shook his head. 'Quite honestly, we don't. No one studies them like that.'

This disconcerted me. I like thinking that there's always an expert who knows everything I don't.

'Is it safer for them to feed at the tip, do you think?' I pressed on. 'I read a Greenpeace article about seabirds who starve to death after eating plastic out in the ocean. Maybe there's more edible food at the landfill?'

Graeme was much more comfortable with ambiguity than me. 'That's a really good question,' he said, 'and another one we don't know the answer to. We don't know what exactly they're eating down there, let alone what that food does to them.' He seemed drawn to this question now. 'How are they processing it? How are their bodies adjusting? It's not high quality.' He looked down at his hands and then up at me. 'At a colony near Lake Rotorua, I once saw a chick regurgitate an entire string of sausages. An *entire* string.'

Robert is also realistic about everything we don't know about the tip flock's future but agrees that, like in any ecosystem, their fate is tethered to the landfill's fate.

'What will be most interesting is what happens when tips stop receiving all food waste,' he said. In the last two decades the Southern Landfill has diverted 26 percent of food waste from being buried and he expects that to increase. It's an urgent task if we're going to reduce greenhouse gases: organic materials—kitchen scraps, leftovers, unopened meat trays—generate methane when they degrade underground without oxygen. For the planet's sake, hopefully we'll soon have landfill without food, just construction waste and biosolids, which don't generate methane but neither of which seagulls can eat. Robert and Graeme both speculated that without their main food source, the tip flock might migrate to landfills that still accept food or find other food sources in the city. Maybe their population will shrink. We don't know.

I'll miss the tip flock if they disappear. I have the tip face to thank for the stray gulls I see playing in the wind out my kitchen window every day, catching updrafts and bouncing off the hills for fun.

'What will happen to the tip itself?' I asked Robert. The Southern Landfill's consents expire in 2026 and decisions loom in the city council chamber. They'll likely just open up more land nearby to fill with waste.

'Once it's full, it'll get capped and then permanently monitored,' he said. 'Capping' landfill means flattening the waste, spreading thick layers of dirt and topsoil on top, then planting turf. Robert and his team manage thirty-five ex-landfill sites in Wellington.

'Here's a thing,' he said, suddenly. 'Where do you live?'

'Berhampore, near Newtown.'

'You know MacAlister Park? That's capped landfill.' He thought for a second. 'And the soccer field by Toi Whakaari? Also, ex-landfill. It's ironic but often we only get public parks thanks to landfill.'

Flat land has always been at a premium in Wellington, so gets gobbled up quickly by commercial development. Only old landfill—potentially toxic and unreliable to build on—is worthless enough to be left for social purposes. In the city, if you find yourself in a flat, open, public, green space, it's almost certainly ex-landfill. The signs are obvious if you know how to look, Robert said: Central Park, Tawatawa Reserve, the Botanic Garden, all of Houghton Valley. Even the airport is built on ex-landfill.

So soon enough, the Southern Landfill will go quiet. It will become an improbably flat, green, open space among Wellington's hills. People will walk their dogs or play sports. Maybe kids will boogie board across the puddles that form where the ground gently buckles. Gulls will always gather there, shuffling from foot to foot in a storm above the ghost tip. Gull and landfill permanently and inextricably tied together on the south coast.

When I told Graeme about my favourite birds at MacAlister Park, we started cataloguing the other flocks we found interesting around the city.

'Have you ever seen the washing flock down at Ōwhiro Bay?' he asked.

I nodded. 'Yeah, when I go for walks past the tip. Ōwhiro

Bay is only a bit after the turn-off. I've often wondered what that flock is up to or where they've come from.'

At the beach, the Ōwhiro stream meets Te Moana-o-Raukawa. Just out in the bay, a huge flock of tarāpunga and karoro engulf the sea and sky. Hundreds of birds bob on the ocean or swirl above it, uttering caws that I'd lately begun to interpret as mournful. Luckily, my assumption was wrong. Graeme, with his expert eye, knows an ordinary birdy day when he sees one.

'It's the perfect place for gulls,' said Graeme. 'They probably get a bit grubby at the landfill, so at Ōwhiro Bay they can wash in the stream, have a bit of a drink, get something more to eat and continue home.'

That's how I choose to think of the tip flock now, splashing about in brackish water, ridding themselves of human muck and flying home, full.

Meccanoman

On a Saturday afternoon in mid-March, the train ride out of Wellington is impossibly beautiful. Hundreds of black swans bob in Porirua harbour and Kāpiti Island dozes in the sun. Except for the tiny tick of other people's lives, the train is quiet. For a while I listen to two teenagers analyse their classmates' Instagrams but they rush off the train at Plimmerton, and as it pulls away I see the taller one snort her milkshake onto the platform. Both girls shriek and laugh. The woman across from me removes the price stickers from three cellophane-wrapped bunches of gerberas before alighting at Paraparaumu. Eventually I'm alone in the carriage, the only person going all the way to Waikanae and the New Zealand Federation of Meccano Modellers biennial convention.

Meccano is an Edwardian toy that resembles complex mechanical Lego. Its basic components are small, perforated metal strips and plates, painted in either fire-engine red or forest green. They represent the weighty beams and struts of real-life construction, aspiring to a gravitas that says 'skyscraper suitable', but with Meccano you use the strips and plates to build miniature working replicas of bridges, tanks, diggers and ride-on lawn mowers—maybe a truss that would be useful for mice. A Meccano set also contains hundreds of nuts, bolts and familiar-looking bits with unusual names: pinion, bracket, axle rod, flanged wheel, fishplate, bevel gear, crank handle. It comes with mini screwdrivers and mini spanners. Meccano is civil engineering at the scale of clockwork.

Outside the Waikanae Memorial Hall, a banner flaps in the wind like a heraldic standard. *Meccano: more than just a hobby!* Me: a decent daughter!

I push through two sets of glass doors and step into the building. Inside, it looks like a cinderblock high-school gym, camouflaged with forty trestle tables and manly bunting. The room emits the genial hum of a busy school gala, and every inch of every table is jam-packed with models. For people who value scale and accuracy, the Meccano modellers have given very little thought to an organising principle. Just to my left, a five-foot-tall Eiffel Tower tussles for space with *Kaye's Funicular Railway!* and two French knitting machines that spew woollen cord onto the floor. The HMS *Vanguard*, a metre-long warship slicing through the waves of a blue minky blanket, bumps up against *Dr Meccano*, a child-sized 'robot' that offers juddering, mechanised 'podiatry services' by tickling your feet with a toothbrush.

The NZFMM uniform is a green polo shirt and red cap and, wandering around with my overnight bag, I immediately mistake two different men for my father. I am lost in a forest of distracted dads, of bald spots, potbellies and belted blue jeans. None of them looks at me as I walk past. Instead, they lean over their models and I hear them sigh, stooped with a mini screwdriver, as they recalibrate their 1:400 replica of a German U-boat or John Deere front-end loader.

Finally, I spot my actual father tinkering with something that looks like a scale model of a CNC router, a table-mounted power tool for cutting wood.

'Hello, my darling,' he says, reaching out to pat my arm. 'Hold on a tick, I'll just give Gavin back this Phillips-head.'

My father, Richard, is a man of ordinary height. He has reassuringly broad shoulders, like he would envelop you in an earnest hug, and the thick midriff of someone who calls vegetables 'rabbit food'. In his forties, he broke his back falling from a tree and now, three decades later, his lower back still doesn't work so well. He walks quite slowly and stiffly, as if his feet might not carry him to where he needs to be, but I have never heard him complain about the dull ache in his spine, and he slugs handfuls of medication every morning without a peep. In my whole life, I have never seen him without a beard. Richard mainly reads sci-fi novels and always texts me when there's a moon landing.

When I was five, my friend Rachel was terrified of Richard. These were the years when his hair fell around his face in wild black curls and he shouted if you bumped the computer while skipping past. Rachel didn't have a dad of her own, though, so she didn't know that dads were just like that or that Richard could be extremely polite too, because he was from a farming town in Rangitīkei and he lived at boarding school from the age of six. At seventy-three, Richard's curls are gone and his grey hair is clipped to a Number 3. He always has reading glasses perched on his head. I noticed recently he's much softer as an older man. When did he change? I thought, startled. I couldn't imagine him roaring at his grandchildren for skipping too vigorously. Instead I watched, incredulous, as Richard spent half an hour showing my nephew, at a four-year-old's pace, how to run the model trains he keeps in the garden. When my nephew crashed Thomas the Tank Engine into a shrub, my dad just fished it out, laughing, and explained yet again that *we accelerate* safely *around corners.*

The Meccano model he's exhibiting is a kind of drawing machine named *The Digital Meccanograph.* It's an update on an analogue model from 1928, a proto-Spirograph that drew geometric designs and roulette curves. Richard's digital version is much more complex. It uses similar principles to a CNC router, except, instead of cutting wood, *The Digital Meccanograph* uses a Sharpie to draw pictures he's downloaded from the internet. It's hooked up to a very old laptop that, Richard tells me later, is perfect because 'serial ports have exactly the right voltage for stepper motors'. I smile, grateful for how he speaks to me, his assumption that I understand what he's saying. I do know what a serial port is, but I've never seen a stepper motor or considered how you corral voltage.

Together we watch as the Sharpie moves deftly around a piece of paper. It draws a lion and unicorn, in shiny metallic gold, underneath a flag that reads *NZFMM CONVENTION 2021.*

'Wow. This is awesome,' I say, and then, 'Can I take this home?' gesturing at the piece of paper.

'Of course, honey,' says Richard. This mechanical internet art will look great on my fridge.

While Richard carefully extracts the picture, I can hear his partner, Julie, telling a man and his young son that *The Digital Meccanograph* is 'Meccano meets computers! Meccano goes DIGITAL!' She has jotted the note *X, Y plotter* on her hand

and is gesturing passionately. The man is nodding; the wee boy wide-eyed. They all erupt into laughter.

Among her many gorgeous qualities, Julie is truly the best of sports. She is tall and athletic, a founding member of her walking group and a gardening devotee. Whenever we visit, Julie and Pat spend hours discussing Japanese anemones or how to nourish cuttings. Richard and I talk about orreries or the small motion-activated catapult he's made to shoo cats from their fishpond. We also talk a lot about my job as a digital archivist, where I spend hours copying files from scratched CD-Roms, last used in 1994.

Julie and Richard have been together since they were both in their mid-sixties. The habits of thought and the inevitably eccentric routines each developed over their lives don't seem to have created a barrier to their love: they have splashed into each other's lives with abandon. Julie has got Richard in a pub quiz team, playing bowls, inviting his children to stay, and acting as official photographer for her choir. In turn, she comes to Meccano meetings and astronomy club. She encourages Richard, even as his G-gauge train set encroaches on her beloved garden. I sense that their differences bond them and allow them to be impressed by each other. Sometimes I overhear them gossiping, bringing each other news from their days.

According to their website, the NZFMM was founded in the 1970s by a group of 'Meccanomen throughout the country, each with a deep interest in Meccano as a hobby, and a passion for making models'. Five major clubs span the country. My dad is a member of the Whanganui–Manawatū–Taranaki branch and he also edits the *NZFMM Magazine*. The Meccanomen are almost all exactly that—

men—almost all Pākehā, and almost all retired. Their name tags say Gavin, Reg and Terry. Before retiring, many of the Graemes and Alistairs worked as sewing-machine mechanics, electrical engineers and railway inspectors.

Richard was a radiologist. He worked mainly in nuclear medicine, a specialised area of radiology that uses minuscule amounts of radioactive chemicals to diagnose organ problems. Part of the reason why I think he suits being a Meccanoman is that he never lost his love for finely calibrated scientific instruments, like CT scanners and sonographs. When I was six, I wrote a story called 'My Daddy' and illustrated it with a picture I'd cut out from the *Evening Post*. In it, Richard stands in his lab coat next to the hospital's new MRI machine. The text of my story read, *my daddy loves me. He likes potatoes. ~~Whenn Whehn we~~ I like him!*

I am very taken with the *Rubik's Cube Solver* entered by David from Wellington. By 'taken with' I mean charmed and a little sceptical that a machine can solve a Rubik's cube. But it makes sense to me that Meccanomen are also Rubik's cube men. It was designed as an educational toy, and used for teaching algebraic theory and meditating on movement and space. Meccano also has that problem-solving, philosophical air. I think the cube has nostalgia points, too: the puzzle swamped world leisure in the 1980s, when New Zealand's Meccanomen had small children and could distract themselves from the monotony of parenthood or idle away time with toddlers by memorising the algorithms to solve it.

David lets me scramble the Rubik's cube into a muddled colourful lump and place it into his rickety contraption. Light sensors record the cube's layout and then two mechanical grabbers pick it up. The grabbers swivel the edges around, backwards and forwards, over and over, so that within a few minutes the cube is back to pristine. Each side is one neat, uniform shade: yellow, white, red, blue, orange, green. I am astonished, humbled.

'It will probably win,' Richard told me. 'It often does. It's even got two thousand hits on YouTube.'

Two prizes are up for grabs over the weekend: a people's choice award, and also the coveted Bruce Baxter Memorial Trophy for Exhibitors' Choice, an award voted on by the Meccanomen themselves. The Bruce Baxter Memorial Trophy winner will be announced at the convention dinner tonight but the people's choice award won't be revealed until late Sunday afternoon.

My dad has always been good in miniature. When I was seven or eight, he wired my doll's house with working lights. At the time, my whole world was Sylvanian Families, dinky animal figurines made from flocked plastic. The human-like cats and badgers wore green overalls or blue gingham dresses, and they lived respectable, middle-class, woodland lives in families of four.

Richard installed three tiny lightbulbs—'grain of wheat' bulbs, he called them—in the plastic A-frame house, two downstairs and one in the attic. I could switch them on and off as I liked and I revelled in the new authenticity of the Badger Family's life. In the evening after dinner, I would stay in the kitchen and turn on the doll's house lights, tinkering away with furniture and watching my mother doing dishes as the sky darkened outside the kitchen window. Down on the floor with my Sylvanian house I could immerse myself in a Sylvanian Family life, a house free of the sadness and strain that simmered away between my own parents.

The doll's house lights worked for a couple years, until maybe a few months after my parents divorced. Something came unstuck or unsoldered and I couldn't fix it. I kept hoping that if I toggled the switch the right number of times, light would flood the rooms again. *On* to *off* to *on* to *off* and *on*. It never worked. And Richard had moved to the Wairarapa to be with someone whom my mother and her friends called 'The Other Woman', so I knew he wouldn't ever have time to repair the switch for three grain-of-wheat lightbulbs.

Walking around the hall with my voting form, I'm beginning to see that there's an implicit hierarchy of Meccanomen, informed by the models they choose to build and how they execute them. Sitting atop the pyramid are modellers who take a particular set—let's say the *1956 Second Edition Ferris Wheel*—and use every piece to build a completely different model, like a historically accurate twelve-pound cannon from the Napoleonic Wars. This Meccanoman has showed resourcefulness, economy, creativity and gumption.

Next come the modellers who build an original Meccano model. Apparently, Meccano changed significantly in 1908 and pieces from the first five years don't work alongside the pieces that came after. If you have a complete set from 1903—over 120 years ago—then you are the historian's Meccanoman. This Meccanoman shows diligence, patience and a tender care for his materials. Over the afternoon, I notice that these modellers overlap with the men who are interested in mechanics for mechanics' sake. The models they build have an abstract purity, and names like *A Reverse Circular Machine* or *A Demonstration of All Gearing Mechanisms*. I suspect these men also love prisms, elegant objects that demonstrate complex principles, chic in the face of the Rubik's cube's colourful fanfare.

Coming in third are the modellers who make anything they want, from any pieces, of any set they like. These men are artists, but often have immense technical skill. Improvisation is a risky move but these Meccanomen can suddenly leap to the top, stepping over their club mates with one colossal stride, depending on the ambition of their vision and the resulting complexity of the model. At the last competition the Bruce Baxter Memorial Trophy was won by *Meccanoland*, a sprawling mouse-sized theme park that included not just a working Ferris wheel but roller coasters, a ghost train *and* a white elephant stall. This year, Alistair from Christchurch has eschewed mechanisation altogether and built his own interpretation of St George and the Dragon. I twitch with surprise at how the red Meccano plates, ever so slightly out of context, conjure the flaming belly of a monstrous beast. 'I didn't have a piece that would work for St George's helmet,' Alistair explains, 'so I cut up my wife's measuring spoons.' I tell him that the tablespoon helmet is very convincing.

This zone of extreme risk and reward is where Richard builds his models. This is the testing ground for *The Digital Meccanograph*.

At a distant last, still lacing up their shoes in the dust while others run away, are modellers who make a contemporary model, built directly from an instruction pamphlet, 'like Lego'. These people are not considered serious contenders, and they may not have understood what Meccano is all about.

All afternoon *The Digital Meccanograph* churns out picture after picture. I see several repeat visitors requesting new images. Richard always makes sure to ask little kids what they want the machine to draw.

One child, fidgeting from foot to foot, squeaks, 'A photo of my family?'

Richard smiles. 'That's a great suggestion, but I'm sorry to say this can only draw pictures from the internet. How about I draw you a gazelle? And would you like to know how it works?'

The kid nods his head and my dad puts more paper in *The Digital Meccanograph*. We all watch as a bright green gazelle emerges. The kid is mesmerised while Richard explains, as best he can to an eight-year-old, how software turns the picture into series of x and y coordinates. The Sharpie, attached to a moveable drawing arm, just follows them in sequence. The coordinates are so finely distributed, and the Meccanograph's mechanics so precise, that the binary signal bleeping into the machine flows from the Sharpie as a smooth, uninterrupted line. The kid nods solemnly. I admire how my father has rendered visible this tiny transformation from digital to analogue. These words are usually just abstract concepts, ways of describing how information is exchanged, but Richard has made them tangible, left them gently on the trestle table for everyone to interrogate and understand.

This is where my father truly shines—in this unholy union of practical and absurd. *The Digital Meccanograph* draws beautiful pictures but comes with very little practical purpose. Like four tiny mops attached to cat-sized socks or a Rube Goldberg machine, its ornateness subverts its own utility. Why not just buy a printer if you want pictures? But this is Richard's whole energy, as if practicality ruins the joy of exploring ideas. For him, understanding the world and being able to render abstract knowledge artfully legible is more important than finding useful applications for what you learn. My favourite Meccano model of his demonstrates deep time—or, more specifically, our inability to understand time on a geological scale. It would fit inside a shoe box and looks simple: just a series of different cogs attached to one another in sequence. But the way he's connected them means that each cog rotates more slowly than its neighbour. By the final gears, even as you keep merrily winding the early cogs, the device seems to cease turning completely. It turns out you must turn the first cog for three million years for the final cog to rotate just once.

After he left the family, Richard moved further and further away, from the Wairarapa to Whanganui to Taranaki, and after a year or two we stopped having much to do with each other. The Other Woman didn't care for his children, was suspicious and wary of us. She called us uncivilised when we drank straight from the taps and at the stilted dinner table she once hissed at my father, 'I think Humphrey is *stealing* from me.' After two disastrous visits to their place, my brothers and I were never invited back.

Months, and then years, passed as they do in difficult family relationships: cancelled plans, increasing scepticism, no one saying what they mean, distance. As a teenager, I was also too preoccupied with my mother's pain to notice that I didn't have much to do with Richard and by the time I was at university, I was indifferent to the word 'father'. Even when I did see him it felt like an alien sound, with no relation to expectations or actions. It was a tiny, resentful stone I had to swallow.

The shift in our relationship was such a gradual unfolding that, looking back, I'm unable to pinpoint the moment we were officially 'in touch' again. I guess a thaw starts slowly. What seems like a single drop of water is followed by a second, and then a third. I don't remember Richard saying that he was divorcing his second wife, but sometime in 2011 all the tiny disruptions to my mostly father-free life appeared too regularly for me to dismiss as coincidence. A forwarded Dilbert cartoon; a question in G-chat, have you heard about the library job yet; a text message sent from Rufus's house in Sydney, your new nephew is very cute.

That year, I saw him in Taranaki for the first time in a decade because, now that he was divorced, I could visit his house again. The two of us drove out to the coast and went for a walk on the beach.

'Should we collect some sand?' Richard offered. 'I think I've got some jars in the car. This stuff is great fun, it's magnetic.'

Back at his house I poured Taranaki's black iron grit onto sheets of cardboard while Richard found us some magnets. It was easy because magnets emerge like loose change at his house; they pop up in the cutlery draw or down the side of the sofa, all shapes and sizes. We spent hours making elaborate designs using the sand, drawing it around the cardboard in swirls and swishes, even identifying magnetic north. I'd left Wellington intending to have zero fun in Taranaki but, despite myself, I liked spending time with Richard. I'd forgotten how interesting he was, how much I liked learning that polar north and magnetic north were different. When it rained, I lay on the couch and read *Middlemarch* while he repaired a computer. He brought me cups of tea and biscuits.

That September, we had dinner when he came to Wellington for a work trip. I'd just broken up with my boyfriend and tears escaped over tapas as I told him about it. He squirmed and was silent at the other side of the table, unsure what to say or how to acknowledge my pain beyond patting me uneasily on the arm. But the next day he brought me a Kindle to my flat. 'Maybe you'll have more time to read, now?' he said.

There are a surprising number of wives at the Meccano convention. They sit next to their husbands, silent and calm with glasses and grey bobs. They wear polar fleece zip-up tops from Postie Plus in raspberry or baby blue and, while their Meccanomen reattach pinions or explain words like 'torque' to children, they knit.

The occasional wife has entered her own model. I ask a woman called Ruth if she's entered anything.

She blushes. 'Oh—it's—only this rally car. But it's a recent model. And I made it from the booklet. Graeme's ride-on mower is completely made up. He copied it from the John Deere website.'

'I *like* the rally car, Ruth,' I say. She blushes again.

I write RALLY CAR: *entry 14.2* in second position on my voting form, after *The Digital Meccanograph*, then decide to give my remaining votes to women entrants only. I add *Kaye's Funicular Railway!* and a walking spider the size of a dachshund made by a woman called Cherry, who turns out to be married to the current national president, Lyall. She wears her Air Force name tag and NZDF decorations high up on her polo shirt. Even though she retired from Ohakea several years ago she still speaks with Defence Force clarity. 'You just missed some children—six or seven of them— enthralled—by the spider.'

I nearly stumble into the spider on the floor and Cherry

leans back in her chair, looking at me with her long arms folded. Her face challenges me to do that again. I do not.

Alongside Ruth, Kaye and Cherry there is only one other woman to vote for. She is also the only woman my age at the whole convention, with a glossy high ponytail that tumbles down her back and beautiful sculpted Instagram eyebrows that look out of place against the real 'ear hair' vibe of the room.

'How did you get into this?' I ask Molly over the top of her model swing set. She grins at me as she demonstrates how to make the swing seats move by turning a crank. She wanted to automate the movement but her stepper motor had too much . . . torque.

'I married into it,' she says, and cocks her head towards her husband, Keegan, who is deep in conversation with his father, Keith. Keegan and Keith are consulting a book called *101 Great Tanks*.

World War Two is a recurring preoccupation at the NZFMM convention. I notice that many of the modellers, alongside their main competition piece, have also entered small military models. Their name plaques read *German Railway Mounted Gun* or *WW2 Floating Crane*. These models sit quietly next to the louder, clacking, showier pieces. Out of respect, no guns or tanks include LEDs. Instead, they are an unspoken thread criss-crossing the whole room, as if it's the one category all the men can share, maybe where their modelling skills can be compared on a level playing field.

Richard's father, like many, fought in North Africa during World War Two. He was captured as a prisoner of war in Poland and my grandmother, left at home with a toddler, didn't know for years if her husband was alive or dead. My uncle, the toddler, didn't meet his father until he was six.

My own father was born after the war, once the family was uneasily reunited. When my grandfather came back, he remained permanently taciturn. It's the familiar story of a traumatised person who didn't know how to process what he experienced. He returned to his job as a rural doctor, didn't discuss the war, drank a bit much, and built Meccano with his sons when they were allowed breaks from boarding school.

I gaze around the room and wonder what else, what other silences and questions, the Meccanomen grapple with.

Once, when Julie went on a girls' trip to the World of Wearable Art in Wellington, Richard stayed behind in New Plymouth to potter in the garage and finish his scale model of a New Zealand Railways Department cottage. It would sit next to the train tracks where they carved a path through Julie's alstroemeria.

On the Sunday night he felt tired and not up to his usual concentration. Bad heartburn had kicked in after dinner and he needed to go to bed early. A little later, Richard was choked awake by pain suffocating his chest. A cricket chirruped in his medically trained ear. *Oh,* he thought, *I should call myself an ambulance.*

My brother had to ring me at work the next day. The office blinds were lowered against the late afternoon sun, and I could see a colleague dithering by the photocopier.

'Flor—where are you?' Henry sounded uncharacteristically serious.

'I'm at work. Why? What's going on?' I asked, clambering off my chair onto the floor so no one would hear me.

'Richard's had a heart attack. He got airlifted to Waikato Hospital last night.'

'Last night? Fuck. Is he . . . okay? Who told you?'

'He's alive. He's having surgery tomorrow. Julie rang me and asked if I'd ring you and Ru and Humph. He wasn't there when she got home.'

'Fucking hell, Hen,' I said, no longer whispering.

'I know.'

'Have you talked to him?'

'No,' said Henry, 'he forgot to take his phone charger in the ambulance.'

I left work early and caught the bus home among the jangling noise of schoolkids, crying as quietly as possible behind my sunglasses. There were two goth kids pashing violently in the seat in front of me, smearing lipstick around each other's mouths. Though we had reached a truce, and I felt more at ease with having a father than I had in my early twenties, Richard and I still didn't talk very often. I didn't often bother to be honest with him about how I felt or share my real opinions, which felt the same as not allowing him to know me at all. The distance between us felt cavernous and hollow, if at least mercifully laced with affection.

'It's buzzy to me,' I say to Richard, when I return to his table, 'that there are so many wives here. I feel like wives *my* age wouldn't give up their whole weekend just for their husband's hobby. Don't they have their own lives?'

My dad doesn't look up from refilling *The Digital Meccanograph* with paper. He has a pencil in his mouth and his voice comes out crooked.

'Maybe they like being here, darling. Maybe it's the only time they get to spend with their husbands.' Richard finishes installing the paper, takes the pencil out of his mouth. 'Things are different when you're seventy-five.'

I don't say anything, feeling the tug of his gentle reproach like a sinker attached to a fishing line. I want to laugh at myself, too, because I know he's right.

'Why don't you go and say hello to Terry Curlew?' he suggests.

'Pa,' I say, 'Terry doesn't like me. Remember?' Richard laughs, but I persist. 'He thinks I'm uppity because I'm into gender diversity.'

I look across the room, where I can see Terry wrestling with his *Ping-Pong Ball Machine!* It should briskly chip a line of ping-pong balls into a basket but instead it is jettisoning them all over the floor. Terry is swearing and shouting, adamant that the calibration went skew-whiff on the drive down. I text Pat: Terry's ping pong ball machine isn't working. It's throwing them all over the floor. Pat replies almost instantly: Dare I say...hahaha?

Pat and I met Terry and Sue Curlew when we visited Richard and Julie a few years ago. Over the cheese and crackers, Terry kept talking over Sue in a way I found appalling, but the argument we eventually had was over pronouns. Terry started it. I'd been willing to remain silent—complicit, even—in his Sue-shushing because they'd been married for fifty-two years and the shushing was their business. But then Terry offered his thoughts on 'young people these days' and I took the bait. Why do old men always want to goad women in their thirties? And *why* does Terry mind who goes by they/them? Terry and I snarked at each other for fifteen minutes, ruining the perfectly nice platter of cheese and crackers for everyone else.

In bed that night, Pat suggested that Terry sensed his Rotarian power waning and wanted to take it out on the nearest woke leftie. He didn't have any real control in the world anymore so he made robots and baited his friends' daughters. I agreed, and made a mental note to apologise to Richard about arguing with his friend. I would also thank him for his serenity about changing attitudes towards gender. His obsession with the world in miniature seemed to have left him more at ease ceding control on bigger issues.

At the convention, though, I still feel quietly self-righteous about millennial-style marriage and gratified that Sue hasn't condescended to sit by Terry all weekend. Instead, she's taken her e-bike to Pekapeka.

After his heart attack, I got through to Richard during the night, after Julie arrived at his ward and brought his phone charger. Apparently, she was *never ever going to the fucking World of Wearable Art ever again.*

'Pa? It's me,' I said. 'I wanted to check that you're okay?'

Richard breathed out a long way. 'Oh my darling,' he said, and then his voice wobbled. 'It's so good to hear you.'

I realised that Richard was crying. Holding the phone, my fingers shook and I couldn't reply for a few seconds. I had never heard him cry, not when he left our family, or when he broke his back, or when he met his first grandchild.

'You must have been so scared Pa,' I said, wishing I could be there to bring him a cup of tea and a biscuit. '*I* was really scared—I can't lose you,' I confessed.

Richard had surgery the next morning. They put stents in his coronary artery: two tiny stainless-steel tubes in his heart.

'Just imagine the smallest water pipe you've ever seen,' he said over the phone later, 'only millimetres in diameter. It gets put in the artery, compressed, and they inflate it with a tiny balloon.'

'Wow that seems super intricate.'

'Oh, it really is. And they let me watch the surgery too.'

'They . . . let you watch the surgery?'

'Yeah, they put the X-ray screen where I could see. It was wonderful.'

Stents are installed using a catheter, a wire shaped like a miniature shepherd's crook, my dad told me. They inserted the crook into the veins in his thigh and guided the stents all the way up his torso, into his heart, where they inflated the pipe. Veins don't have any nerve endings—'They're insensate,' Richard said—so he couldn't feel anything. Watching the surgeon guide the stents using X-ray, my dad was one of few patients able to understand what was happening. He knew the name of each vein the catheter travelled through as it moved up his body.

'Well, I'm glad it was at least interesting?' I said, laughing.

At the convention dinner, while people tuck into lamb roast, Des Hogan, the very-newly elected National President, announces that Terrence from Levin has won the Bruce Baxter Memorial Trophy for his working model *A Rotary Wheel Excavator*. Terrence wears a train driver's cap and has a trim white beard. He stands, in his trout-fishing vest, bow-legged and barely as tall as me. He is very shy in the face of this accolade from his peers.

'This idea for a model came to me by accident,' he whispers. 'I saw an abandoned digger on TV, rusting in a field in the former East Germany, and I wondered . . . I wondered, could I build that digger?'

The room erupts into applause, amidst shouts of *outstanding* and *so well-deserved*.

I am sitting between Julie and a serene woman whose husband exhibited a Meccano power-loom. It clacked away in the corner weaving cloth all afternoon. Chatter hums around us from every table; no one can stop talking about the afternoon's AGM. Apparently, there was a coup.

'Des Hogan's been ringing round the branches for months,' Julie explains, 'convincing everyone to vote for him for president, not Lyall again.'

The serene woman nods. 'My Hugh said the same thing.'

As we leave the dinner, I wave goodbye to Lyall and Cherry.

Cherry gives a sharp nod. 'See you at 0800 hours.'

After we get back to Richard and Julie's Airbnb, I sit up with my dad in the kitchen. Julie's going to bed early, and they give each other a big hug, murmuring *goodnight* and *I love you*. 'You were so great today . . . thanks for being so great today,' Richard says to her.

Julie waves him away, shaking her head with gentle disbelief. 'I had lots of fun, love,' she says, and then kisses his cheek before leaving the room. She'll spend the second day of the convention walking the Escarpment Track with Sue Curlew.

Richard sips limoncello from a tiny glass that makes his hands looks huge. He tells me about his best friend in Meccano club. 'He's a retired electrical inspector. And a lovely bloke. He builds *breathtaking* models. I mean, meticulous doesn't even come into it. All the screws face the same way.'

'Wow,' I say, and take a sip of my limoncello. The moon over Kāpiti Island looks like a giant radiant shell. 'Do you have any . . . enemies?' I ask.

'Roger,' sighs Richard and I'm surprised by his answer because I was kind of joking.

'Oh, shit. Okay. Roger? Is he in your club?'

'Yeah, he was the branch treasurer when I joined. I think he felt frustrated when I signed up and wanted to take Meccano digital.'

'What happened?' I asked.

'Last year we had a competition to build a famous artwork—you'll remember, I built that 1:400 *Angel of the North*?' I nod. 'Roger built a statue and then he said it was *me*. But it was—well, it was grotesque, actually. Horrific. An ogre.'

'Jesus, Pa. That's awful. I'm sorry.'

'Oh, it was awful . . . it really was.'

'But you're grown adults. Old men, even.'

He takes another sip of limoncello, looks down at the table, sighing. 'Sometimes I think we're still just little boys.'

I pat his arm and smile at him, until he looks up and returns my smile. We're silent for a moment and watch the moon hover out the window.

'You could write something about the Meccano convention for the magazine if you wanted. You know—an outsider's perspective?' he says. 'I'd love to read more of your writing.'

'Maybe,' I say. 'But I'd probably write about the gender pols of Meccano club.'

'Of course,' says my dad.

'I don't think Terry would ever forgive me,' I say.

The next morning Richard gets up early, takes his mini screwdrivers, and goes to the hall to recalibrate *The Digital Meccanograph*. I'm asleep when he leaves but I stop in on my way back to the train station. No one is at his trestle stand. The man from the table next door strides over to me and sticks his hand out; his pink cheeks gleam in the hall's fluorescent lighting.

'Des Hogan. National president, elect.' He points to his table a few metres away. 'Built that rotary hoe, entry 40.3.'

'Hi,' I say, 'Flora—Richard's daughter.'

Des guffaws. Heartily. 'And here I was thinking you belonged to Brian over here! I wanted to say, *Well you don't get your looks from him!* But you really don't, hah!'

I smile politely. 'No, I get my smarts from that guy, though.' I point at my dad, who is finally walking back to the trestle table with his cup of notoriously milky coffee. 'I'd better go and say goodbye before I miss the train. Nice to meet you though.'

'See you at the next one,' says Des, still chortling.

I pause, stumped by what feels so meaningful in this silly conversation. Then I click: I can't remember the last time I got to introduce myself like that. As Flora, Richard's daughter.

On the train home, the old man across the aisle from me exfoliates his elbows with pumice and I eavesdrop on a man about my age who is wearing a hunting jacket and gumboots. He slugs back a blue Powerade and makes increasingly agitated phone calls. The weeds lining the tracks are blossoming into a wall of purple and before we even reach Paekākāriki station I am crying, as quietly as possible behind my sunglasses.

Even now, with the empty years behind us and me finally fully aware that I like and respect my dad, I am still startled by proximity to him. How do people who see their dads often do this? How do they tolerate this feeling? Inside my chest, it is as if the smallest container, a bottle cap or a thimble, is bigger than it was at first glance. As if instead of holding droplets it contains a whole sea, swirling and rolling, gathering power from a deep, broad, unseeable current.

It is into this spray I imagine the HMS *Vanguard* would set sail, off its minky blanket and into the early morning sunshine, beyond Kāpiti Island.

Much later that day, pottering at home, I will get a text that says, hey – I got 2nd prize in people's choice! My highest award ever. Thanks for your ballot stuffing! Rubiks Cube came 3rd.

I will reply, omigosh congratulations. Are you pleased? I'm pleased! And then: also I only voted for you once so that was all your own work Pa 💚💚💚.

The HEA

The queue outside Island Bay New World snaked all the way around the carpark and I stood right at the end, near the back entrance to Island Bay's only dive bar and the fish 'n' chip shop. All around me Wellingtonians in face masks scrolled on their phones or jiggled their reusable shopping bags and bounced from one foot to the other. A message from Pat flashed onto my phone: **Hey we're out of peppermint tea too.** Just ahead of me someone lowered their mask to vape, glancing around. I looked up every so often from my book so I didn't get clipped by a reversing car.

I was reading *Digging Deep* by Jay Hogan, a 2019 novel that tells the story of Caleb Ashton, a raffish commitment-phobe cop, who falls for Drake Park, the only male midwife in Northland. They meet after Caleb arrests Drake at an anti-mining protest in Whangārei. The novel is narrated by both men in alternate sections but it opens with Drake's idealistic, strident voice: 'I'd be damned if I was gonna stand by and let the government sell pristine fucking conservation land out from under our feet without a hell of a fight.'

From Caleb's point of view Drake is a 'cute as fuck midwife with a sting in his tale'. He has 'chocolate eyes'. From Drake's point of view, Caleb is '*holy shit . . . wow* six-foot-three, top-to-toe thirtysomething deliciousness'. He has 'dancing hazel eyes'. *Digging Deep* sits within two sub-genres of romance fiction: 'contemporary' and 'mm', which is written lowercase but pronounced em-em and stands for 'male on male'. At heart, mm novels tell stories of queer men falling in love.

While I stood in the line of shoppers, Drake cooked Caleb dinner: poached chicken and mango stir fry on quinoa. It was their first real date. Inevitably, one thing led to another—a hand brushed across a thigh, a ripe glance—and they had sex. 'Kissing Drake was like opening the best present on Christmas day, the one you've had your eye on under the tree for weeks.' I shuffled a few steps forward in the queue. Drake pulled on Caleb's boxer briefs, 'giving him a front row seat'. I stepped aside for someone and their trolley. Drake 'released a strangled groan'. Up ahead, a small kerfuffle erupted as someone tried to cut the line. Caleb and Drake snuggled on the couch, panting after the exertion, high colour in their cheeks.

In 2019 *Digging Deep* was a finalist in the Gay Romance category of the Lambda Literary Awards—the world's most prestigious queer book awards—and I'd picked it up from the free-book table at the Romance Writers of New Zealand conference ('Love Finds a Way') a few weeks earlier. This conference is the largest gathering of professional and amateur romance writers in Aotearoa. Some people are surprised that this country has such a strong romance fiction community, but we do. The guild that runs the conference, Romance Writers of New Zealand (RWNZ), was established in 1999 by just ten Auckland writers, but in the decades since has grown to four hundred members and eight local chapters around the country. Every two years the whole organisation comes together for two full-up days of writing and business workshops, author presentations and networking. Literary agents are available for pitches. It caters to writers fine tuning their craft as well as beginners only just dipping their toes into the jacuzzi.

'So, where's the conference? Where am I dropping you off?' Pat had asked me that morning, eyebrows raised over a cup of tea, as he sat shirtless in bed.

'The James Cook. On the Terrace,' I said, pulling on my jeans, a towel wrapped around my head.

He laughed. 'Yeah it is! That's my girl. You gonna have the buffet lunch?'

'Um, of course. Could it be any other way?'

Later, when he pulled the car over outside the hotel, he leaned over and gave me a kiss.

'Have a good day, honey. I love you.'

'I love you too, sweetheart,' I said and got out of the car.

I was a few steps away when he rolled down the passenger window and shouted from the driver's seat: 'Baby, I forgot to tell you! I'm a secret billionaire!'

'Thank god for that,' I shouted back. 'I was worried!'

I could see him grinning as he started the car.

That first morning, the conference thrummed with energy. Waiting in the registration queue, I spoke with a woman who'd come straight to the conference from her marae AGM. 'How'd the AGM go?' I asked. 'So choice,' she said. 'Between that, and now this, I'm absolutely buzzing.'

Other people were already spilling coffee because they gestured too hard, and cackles tumbled through the crowd. That day I saw more middle-aged women high-fiving than I have ever seen anywhere else and I kept overhearing the phrase 'these are my people'. And it was over a hundred people, almost all of them women, crammed into the sixteenth floor of Wellington's James Cook Hotel. Only three people presented as cis men, though I did see people high-fiving them too.

Despite the warm and excitable air, I felt shy as I slipped the conference lanyard over my head, like an outsider and a wannabe spying on real writers. I didn't understand the acronyms people threw around, like 'HEA', 'mm' and 'mf'. I wasn't even sure what the term 'trope' meant here. Women introduced themselves using the sub-genres they wrote in— sub-genres I didn't even know existed, let alone ever thought about writing. *What heat do you write?* they asked each other. *Are you pitching this weekend?*

I met a woman who had published over seventy books using five different pen names. 'I'm mainly Paranormal, Historic Scotland, Urban Contemporary and Veterinarian,' she said, counting off on her fingers, 'usually with an Enemies to Lovers slant, but lately I've been really excited by exploring Soul Mates.' I nodded, which I hoped might imply that I had read a romance novel set in a vet clinic. All I could think about was how I used to take my cat to the Tasman Street Vet Centre and how, if I thought about it, I wanted love for everyone who worked there.

At the welcome session, the emcee, Caitlin, introduced herself by shouting at the crowd, 'If you know me then you'll know I'm obsessed with dragons!' We gave thunderous applause. Her thick hair was dyed with blue, purple and bright pink stripes. Caitlin's ice-breaker game started with an instruction: 'Stand up if you've had a *New York Times* or *USA Today* best-seller this year.' A handful of women stood up and, with little smiles, waved self-consciously at the room. Someone in sneakers and jeans curtseyed. I recognised a few of these women as the superstars of local romance writing: Nalini Singh, Jayne Castel, Jay Hogan, Steff Green.

Caitlin grinned at the audience. 'Thanks, ladies. You stay standing. Okay—everyone else, stand if you have published a book in the last year.'

About a third of the room pushed back their chairs and stood up. Caitlin asked more questions: Have you finished a manuscript this year? Have you *started* a manuscript this year? Have you written a chapter this year? Have you written a paragraph this year? Eventually the whole room was on their feet, laughing and talking. Caitlin had to shout and wave to get everyone's attention. Later, this game would feel to me like it represented the whole conference, a place where not just the big-name writers are encouraged to take the limelight, but amateurs and enthusiasts offer something too. Apparently, Nalini Singh still goes to the Auckland branch meetings of RWNZ even though several of her books have been reviewed in *O* magazine.

Writing romance fiction is much, much harder than people assume. In an essay published in the *Pantograph Punch*, Alie Benge charted her attempt to write a romance novel, and how, in failing to do so, she recognised that she hadn't understood or appreciated the genre enough to do it justice. Like most of us, she'd accepted the predictable opinion about romance novels: they're sentimental. They reinforce antiquated heteronormative attitudes. They give women unreal expectations about sex. The writing is bad. Hell, who can take a book seriously when it ends with a *happily ever after*—the HEA, as I found out. But in eventually finding 'feminism with Fabio', Benge unravelled for herself the cultural norms (hey, misogyny!) that belittle romance fiction, as well as the people who write and read it.

It seems to be a path that most women interested in romance fiction, both as readers and writers, have to travel for themselves. In her opening keynote, Jayne Castel, who writes Historical and Fantasy romance, talked us through a series of lessons she'd learned over her career. After listing the many inevitable mistakes a new writer makes, she posed a question that literary fiction writers seldom need to ask themselves.

'If you want to write romance you need to consider the question: do I genuinely respect and love this genre?' Castel looked out at the room and paused, slide clicker in hand. She exhaled. 'I kind of hate admitting this but I don't think I took these books seriously, and my readers seriously, when I started out. I didn't know what this genre could *do.*'

Across from me, a young woman with plaits wound around her head and a tiny stripe of baby puke on her shoulder nodded slowly, emphatically. Chin resting gently in her hand, elbow on the table, she looked a little teary.

To plot a romance novel you use tropes, the specific plot and characterisation beats readers come to expect from any genre. I went into the conference barely understanding how they work but it didn't take long to learn the big names: Enemies to Lovers, Secret Billionaire, Secret Baby, Second Chance, Forbidden Love, Stuck Together.

Some tropes become commonly linked. Stuck Together, for example, often goes hand-in-hand with Enemies to Lovers because, after all, how are you going to get two people who don't like each other to spend a lot of time together unless you strand them on the same island? You can also mix 'n' match. Forbidden Love cut with Secret Billionaire cooks a very different flavour novel from Forbidden Love sprinkled with Friends to Lovers.

The beats of romance fiction are finely grained. Underneath the main trope arc, Castel recommended four phases: 1) The Set Up, 2) Falling in Love, 3) Retreating from Love, and 4) Fighting for Love. In Phase 1, for example, the Heroine should meet the Love Interest (LI), or, as he's known in male-on-female (mf) plot lines, the Male Character (MC). This phase contains an Inciting Incident and the subsequent First Conflict, also known as the No Way! At this point we should be 25 percent of the way through the book and it's time for Game Changer #1, usually a steamy kiss—or sometimes sex if your heat level is 3+. Structurally, romance fiction is tight.

Digging Deep is a variation on Enemies to Lovers: when Caleb arrests Drake they are momentarily on opposite sides of the law, and the opening chapter neatly conflates the Inciting Incident and the No Way! Jay Hogan also writes character-driven books, so *Digging Deep*'s momentum and dramatic tension arise from the interactions and misunderstandings between the two men, and the landscape of their inner lives: the will-they-won't-they tension, their hopes and fears for the relationship, Caleb's commitment phobia and Drake's broken heart.

The most difficult section of any arc comes at Game Changer #3, known as 'Dark Night of the Soul' or the

'Black Moment', usually 75 percent through a novel. This incident, often a symbolic death, bridges Phases 3 and 4. In their story, Caleb and Drake must reckon with the impact of Caleb being stabbed on the job. In the tense aftermath of this event, both men's defences go back up. Drake can't risk being hurt again.

Romance novel tropes feel almost like a tongue-in-cheek response to the rigid advice many women receive growing up. We've been taught all these outlandish rules about sex, none of which focus on pleasure, so why not add a few more but make them . . . actually sexy.

A lot of us start lessons early. At six, I was approached in a swimming pool changing room by several teenage girls who were smitten with my fourteen-year-old brother. They'd been watching me and my siblings on the hydro slide. 'What's his name? What's your phone number?' they asked, surrounding me as I stood dripping in my togs. I never felt more separated from my brothers, more alone, than when I had to get changed in the girls' changing room by myself. I dutifully answered and one girl scribbled Henry's name and our phone number on the arm of their leader. 'Thanks,' they said, tossing the word over their shoulders as they walked away.

My mother was furious. 'You do NOT give our phone number to strangers.' But then she exhaled and her expression softened. 'Flora, girls should never ring boys, okay? Men don't like women who chase them.'

At the time I didn't mind this advice, because instead of being concerned with how girls behave, my main goal was to be a boy. Once, a stranger glanced at me and my brothers at an airport, then commented to my mother, 'Wowee, four sons—you must have your hands full!' My chest erupted with joy. Before I could raise my head to smile, my mother gently corrected the man. The smallest one—with the short brown hair and wearing the full Canberra Raiders tracksuit—was, in fact, a girl. The stranger blurted sorry to the *little lady* but my heart still thudded as if it might break free of my body. He thought I was one of them. Even if just for a few seconds, I had convinced someone.

I stopped wearing my Canberra Raiders tracksuit around the time it dawned on me I'd never become a boy. *You don't even really like league,* the local plumber's son spat at me one lunchtime at school. He lived down the road from my family, a skinny kid with a shaved head who devoted himself to rugby league. The girl from up the road, the daughter of a doctor, was a class tourist and playing at boyhood.

Tucking into my buffet lunch, I thought about how often we repeat the romantic stories in our own lives. Second only to a story about how I got arrested the first and only time I tried shoplifting as a teenager, the story I have retold most in my adult life is how I met Pat. If you have a partner, how often have you narrated your backstory to new friends, or colleagues you're trying to make into friends? People are curious about other people's relationships—what beats they hit, their tropes. How you met your partner, when you first said 'I love you', how they proposed, how you proposed, if there was a proposal at all.

A friend of my mother's met her partner on a beach in Rio de Janeiro on the night of 31 December 1999. It was a huge New Year's Eve party, with face paint and bonfires and fireworks. Lauren's and João's eyes locked across the dark beach, as they breathed deep in the sea air. Their last act of the old millennium was a kiss. When they came back to Aotearoa, people worried for them, because you could never get divorced after that origin story. You'd cling to the relationship long after it was done because who could dump anyone they'd met on the beach in Rio at 11.30pm on 31 December 1999? People needn't have fussed though because João and Lauren were a combination of Unexpectedly Thrown Together and Soul Mates.

I wondered what tropes Pat and I matched. Despite what he'd shouted from the car, he was not a Secret Billionaire.

We met at a party when we were both twenty-three, at a dank flat above the Cash Converters and Down Town Local on Cuba Street. It was an old office space crammed with people. The floor stuck to our shoes and we shouted above the music. A rotating party light slowly illuminated the crowd red, blue, green, red, blue, green. Parties at this flat always ended with people throwing bottles out the window onto the street below. Pat had come on a whim, invited by a work friend of my flatmate. He wore a heavy linen jacket—almost like canvas—in a dirty reddish brown, with a hole in one elbow. Standing close in the darkness we self-consciously discussed something we'd both heard on Radio New Zealand. He rolled a cigarette. When he unexpectedly cracked up at something I said, I looked up at him, startled. He smiled back at me, held my gaze, and his mouth twisted a little to hold onto his unsmoked ciggie.

At the 'Sex-Ed for Romance Writers' session, a woman in her fifties asked, 'So, would we say *metal* cock rings are for more experienced people, then?' I'd been admiring her elaborately shirred peasant top from a few seats away.

The facilitator, a young woman named Emma, nodded. 'Yes,' she said, 'some people are total metal fanatics, though.'

'Do they have a latch or anything?' asked someone else, who I couldn't see properly except for a lush cloud of blue hair.

Emma tilted her head. 'Some do and some don't. The simplest can only be taken on and off when the penis is flaccid, so those are the rings we need to be careful with. Most people I'd recommend starting with plastic.'

'Interesting,' Blue Hair said and scribbled some notes down. 'How long should you leave them on?'

Emma looked thoughtful. 'Well, I wouldn't write a scene that has a metal one on for more than fifteen minutes.'

The only man in the room was Emma's tall, silent boyfriend. He'd helped her set up her computer before the session and now sat at the back beaming proudly, long legs stretched out in front of him. I was sitting next to Justine, the woman with plaits I'd noticed at the keynote. We'd plopped down next to each other and said hello, before admitting this was our first conference. We felt out of place as aspirational genre writers, sheepish about not having actually written a book. She had two small kids and lived on the North Shore. This was her first weekend away from her family in two years, with nothing to think about except her writing and what to eat for dinner. The night before the conference she'd ordered room service and watched Olympic show jumping on TV.

The conversation lulled and I raised my hand. 'Has anyone got recommendations for good, sexy scenes that involve an STI check-in?'

Jay Hogan tapped my shoulder and gave me a smile. She was sitting right behind me. 'Try reading mm. After the AIDS crisis, consent and STI checking became an integral part of the sex scenes. I mean, the language used to be horrible, but it's different now.' She shook her head. 'Thank god you don't read characters saying *you clean?* anymore.'

For the rest of the session, the group nutted out practical and ideological problems. Would dildos be anachronistic in the fifteenth century? Answer: no—archaeologists have dug up what they believe to be bone sex toys that could be sixteen thousand years old. Does *Fifty Shades of Grey* pathologise BDSM? Short answer: yes. How many orgasms is it reasonable to describe a heroine having in a single sex scene—three? six?: any number, so long as it seems believable that the sex could enable it. Everyone agreed on the same pet peeve: representations of 'good' sex in books and TV that comprises fifteen seconds of vaginal penetration followed by screaming tides of erotic energy that pierces the heroine's whole body.

Romance writers are, as Benge notes, extremely frank and chill discussing sex. Everyone at the conference could not have been less embarrassed or more curious about the nourishing potential of good sex. At one point, Emma put a diagram of the whole clitoris on PowerPoint and a few people clapped. I swear I heard someone say, 'Ah, there she is!' The received wisdom from romance writers about writing the 'juicy' scenes—both emotionally juicy and sexually juicy— was to 'live your scenes' in your head before you write them.

I noted a question on my paper: *How often are women encouraged to cultivate this kind of internal sexy life, much less let their desire spill out into the world?*

Pat and I didn't become a couple until two years after we met. I'd had a boyfriend at the party above Cash Converters and Pat wanted to leave Wellington in the aftermath of a messy break-up with his girlfriend, Harriet. For a few months after we first met, I would run into him at the university library where I worked and I would curse myself for blushing when he stopped among the shelves to talk to me. But then he moved overseas to teach English in Dalian, where his father was living, on the Liaodong Peninsula. I stayed in Wellington, kept working at the library and broke up with my boyfriend. For a while I dated an unreliable chef who one friend declared 'too mainstream hot' for me. It had seemed auspicious—romantic even—because he'd asked me out by handing a note over the issue desk, but my friend was still right. He was covered in tattoos; I was self-conscious about my irritable bowel syndrome (IBS). He went surfing; I had opinions about *Downton Abbey*. Needless to say, I liked him way more than he liked me. He dumped me on an evening stroll, as he wheeled his bike along the waterfront.

A few days later, seeing me gloomy, my flatmate shared a secret. 'You know who told me they thought you were special?' she said.

I shook my head, silent and miserable.

'Pat.' She grinned. 'He told me before he went to China.'

I was incredulous. 'But he's such a fox!' I squealed. In my diary I wrote, *I can't believe Pat would think twice about me!?*

Eventually, Pat came back to Wellington for a holiday and a huge group of us went to a music festival held out the back of Wainuiomata. On the first night Pat and I walked across a darkened paddock from our tents towards a stage in the forest. We picked our way between guy ropes and abandoned bits of camping gear, bottles and costumes until he looked sideways at me in the dark.

'So . . . I really like you,' he said.

I stopped mid-stride, tried to choke out what I needed to say. 'No no no. Don't say that. We can't do anything because . . . because of Harriet.' Then I scurried away.

While Pat lived in China, Harriet and I had become friends, bonding at parties about being twenty-four and about the hopeless boys who ghosted us (she, too, dated an unreliable chef). Unlike me, though, Harriet liked to stay close with all her ex-boyfriends. They would still do *anything* for her and they were off limits, ladies.

Jayne Castel looked at the audience from the lectern. 'Okay. So *this* is how you package plot twists.' She pressed play on a YouTube clip. 'Here we go. The quintessential juicy scene.'

On the screen, Colin Firth's Mr Darcy walked into a flowery-papered drawing room and confessed, badly, to Jennifer Ehle's Elizabeth Bennet that he 'ardently admires and loves' her. The whole room cheered when Lizzie shot Darcy down. The woman next to me quoted the whole scene word for word.

'In the Regency period, obviously you don't kiss until the wedding, so this is Darcy and Elizabeth's first game changer,' said Castel. I jotted some frantic notes. 'You need to know what's at stake for your characters,' she continued, 'and be able to draw from your own emotional experiences. Otherwise, readers will not be on board. How can you bring the goals of your characters into opposition, with either each other, or their context?'

Romance writers celebrate tropes, but the community also fosters the ingenuity needed to wield them well. As Benge says, 'Tropes are a useable tool; they're an empty vessel that can be filled differently each time . . . There is great skill in taking a second-hand plot and making it new.'

'You have to think about your characters' backstories and how to make them interact with the tropes,' another writer said to me during the 'Compelling Characters' workshop.

'I do their Myers-Briggs, plot their star charts, envisage their wardrobes, ask myself how they're going to transform before I even start writing. Get to know everything about them.'

I realised that the conference energy was intimately connected with the creative energy of these authors. Novel ideas, plot twists and character arcs poured from every workshop. In 'Compelling Characters' one woman, whose guide dog lay at her feet, devised her next heroine in under two minutes. She would be a Grand Prix showjumper who—after a career-ending injury—is a single mother caring for a daughter and running a riding school for disabled children. The baby daddy is her ex-best friend from childhood who she hasn't seen for ten years. He moves in next door with his new fiancée . . . her one-time equestrian rival.

Yet again, the room erupted into applause.

At the music festival, I avoided Pat for two whole days. But on the final night my yearning became so overwhelming that I tracked him down on an emptying dance floor at 4am.

'Hi!' he said, turning around. I was still for a moment, stupefied by being close to him, but then my hand found his, and we stood there, staring at each other. He opened his mouth, and shut it again. I glanced down at our clasped hands.

'Hey—can I explain something to you?' I said, inclining my head towards the door.

We sat alone in a quiet field, gazing at the lights in the distance. The music was a dull roar. I apologised for freaking out.

'I'm so happy you like me,' I said. 'It's the best thing anyone has ever said to me.'

He nodded but I couldn't really read his expression in the dark. I told him that I liked him too, like a lot, but that nothing could ever happen because Harriet was my friend.

We sat in silence for a few moments, still holding hands. Then we kissed.

A few nights after the conference, I talked to my brother Henry on the phone.

'How was the romance writers thing?' he asked.

'Off the hook,' I said. 'I've never been anywhere more welcoming in my life. Everyone just wants you to get writing, right away.'

Henry laughed. 'I am very unsurprised.'

Down the phone I could hear him chopping lettuce and emptying cans of beans into a pot. His family were having tacos for dinner. While he cooked, we talked mostly about how tropes work in our respective favourite genres: sci-fi and romance. I made a clumsy and defensive statement about romance novels being belittled on the basis of spurious and arbitrary societal values. My brother listened intently.

'Well, there's nothing morally wrong with them, but the genre is doing something different than literary fiction. I dunno . . . I want to say it's about friction?' A cupboard door thudded shut. 'It's not a good or bad value judgement or whatever, but they aren't necessarily there to make you wonder about the great existential problems? They're too . . . frictionless.'

I paused. Henry always phrased arguments in ways I wish I'd thought of. I felt he was partly talking about escapism, and I agree that most books with happy endings are inherently escapist. No life chops off at a wedding or a tasteful kiss. I don't think that romance authors would disagree that their novels are escapist, either. At the conference, I heard many people talking about the importance of uplifting and heart-warming stories, especially in the context of the 2020/2021 COVID season.

I don't necessarily agree that we aren't invited to interrogate wider questions within romance fiction, or that there aren't a million different reasons why someone would read a romance novel beyond escapism. Secret Billionaire is gonna hit different depending on whether you're broke or . . . a secret billionaire.

I picked up *Digging Deep* for practical reasons: I had never read a novel where one of the main characters manages a chronic bowel condition. Drake has an inflammatory bowel disease (IBD), Crohn's, and managing this affects his life a lot, both functionally and emotionally—but he's pragmatic and strong. Early in the book, he spends several paragraphs discussing how he structures his midwifery schedule to help him take care of his health. While he is sure about conservation land and supporting the pregnant women of Northland, he is less sure about sex and love after his boyfriend of two years dumped him while he was severely ill and in hospital.

I don't have Crohn's or ulcerative colitis so can't map my experiences exactly onto those in the book, but I wanted to read something that spoke a little to something I do know about. Ever since my early twenties, the way I experience sex and sensuality, and how I feel about my body on any given day, has been shaped by severe IBS, the significantly less-hardcore cousin to IBD. Or, to put it another way: it can be hard to lose yourself in the moment when you're paranoid about sharting.

The way Hogan writes about illness is delightfully unmetaphorical and completely shame-free. I was unsurprised to find out that she, like Drake, has worked in healthcare, in Hogan's case as a nurse, and her writing reflects that. She understands the reality of a chronic condition: it doesn't feel like a metaphor when it's your body. Like Drake, I have spent time frantically searching for the nearest public toilet in Whangārei, and I also have a detailed mental ranking of the safest toilets at work in which to spend twenty minutes. I felt seen by Drake's approach to his illness: the distraction and exhaustion that can come with chronic pain, the tension between seeing aspects of his condition with levity—he cracks some very dark jokes—and his everyday anxieties. Can I really ask my friends to cook me special meals? Is it boring to say yet again that I feel gross today? Chronic conditions make no one any less lovable or any less fuckable, but I haven't always known that about myself, so, like Drake, I had to spend some time figuring it out. At the time it felt like a fairly existential question.

After the music festival, Pat and I went back to Wellington, where rumours of our fling quickly filtered through our circle of friends and acquaintances. Whispers followed me on the dance floor at bars: he's staying at her flat! How could she have betrayed a friend like that? My name was, as another friend put it, 'a real bad word around town'. Apparently, everyone at Paper Bag Princess, Harriet's work, thought I was a horrible person. I really had put bros before hoes, and you just didn't do that if you wanted to keep your rep. I was distraught. I could never buy clothes at Paper Bag Princess again and Harriet wasn't replying to my texts.

I got her answer at the end of Pat's 'holiday'. He had accidentally missed his flight back to China and rang me, a little sheepish, from the airport. 'I thought . . . I might stay in Wellington? And be your boyfriend?' he said. 'Yes,' I said, overjoyed that he hadn't been able to tell 24hr time. But when I saw Harriet a few days later, at a friend's birthday dinner, she wouldn't speak to me or meet my gaze. I knew that would be the last time we were ever invited to the same dinner.

The next day I cried over a coffee across the table from my mother in the Mediterranean Food Warehouse and sadly picked at my gelato. I'd ordered a large trim flat white, which also felt like a defeat because I'd been trying to drink long blacks ever since the unreliable chef had scoffed at my coffee order. My mother ate some of her gelato and looked at me earnestly, her mouth slumped into a small frown.

'Don't worry, honey, great love always fucks someone off.'

I tried to give her a watery smile. Was this Forbidden Love?

In a break-out space, the author T. G. Ayer put up a slide of an elaborate gamer's chair, the AK-K7012-BR. It resembled the interior of a sports car. 'Help yourself out, everyone. Get yourself one of these,' she said, gesturing at the screen. 'Give your back this gift.' A knowing laugh rippled around the room.

Up at the lectern, Ayer continued. A pair of space-age gloves appeared on the screen. 'You should also invest in a good pair of compression gloves. You don't want to ruin your career by getting RSI.'

Romance writing is one of few ways to make a full-time living as a fiction writer and the community is dedicated to health and safety. They spend a lot of time at their computers: many of the women I spoke to wrote five thousand words 'on a good day'. For them, writing is physical and fast, like an embodied practice. If you bring your body, your mind will follow. Some are sprinters, executing ten-minute bursts around full-time work or childcare. Others are marathon runners, who manoeuvre their writing into week-long bootcamps every few months.

Nalini Singh is a middle-distance runner with immense stamina. She works five days a week, and writes for only forty-five minutes of every hour, with a long lunch break. A reformed 'productivity addict' who pulled twelve-hour days, she entreated the audience, 'Please, don't repeat my mistakes. If you want to enjoy writing and support your creativity you have to give yourself downtime.' She paused. 'But it's still important to train yourself into writing, because sometimes you do have to sit down and do it. I listen to rain sounds and that's when I know it's time to write. I have three different playlists. Rain against the window. City rain. Forest rain. Sometimes I even listen to thunder and lightning if I need to.'

I feel very far away from the person I was when I first fell in love with Pat, the sad twenty-five-year-old not eating her gelato. At the time I thought I'd let everyone down, but I now think I just wasn't prepared for the moral complexity of having to put my own desire before the stated aims of another woman.

These days I am comfortable with what I did. In many ways it was so okay for me and Pat to get together: we liked each other a lot; we were both single; it was a music festival. But I also think Harriet's anger was completely legitimate, whatever its root cause. She'd been hurt by Pat, and I walked over her still-tender feelings. Maybe she still loved him and held out hope, who knows.

At the time, though, I desperately needed people to like me and I craved Harriet's absolution. I thought I couldn't forgive myself until she forgave me so I squirmed with discomfort and guilt for years, much longer than I needed to, because she simply never replied to my texts ever again. It took me a long time to realise that it was possible to step, with very specific purpose, into a moral grey area and own your choices, even if afterwards you're effectively banned from Paper Bag Princess.

Ten years later there is absolutely nothing Forbidden about my and Pat's Love: it is sanctioned by the state, heteronormativity and every single one of our friends and family. My friendship with Harriet ended, but many of my good friends remain close with her and we see each other from time to time at weddings and farewell parties. She stopped working at Paper Bag Princess. My retail exile is over. And Pat gave up smoking in 2017—I haven't seen him roll a cigarette in six years.

Pat's and my origin story has also been annexed by the forces of long-term love. It is completely overwhelmed by everything that's happened in the decade since. Three flats, a house, a cat, a wedding, sobriety. Thousands of meals and orgasms. Tens of thousands of text messages. How many millions of words have we said to each other? In how many different ways? Offhand, furious, diligent, devoted, critical, unthinking. I could probably fill an 80,000-word novel with every instance of the question 'D'you want a cup of tea, bub?'

Like the flatness some people associate with romance novels, history dulls our story, reduces it to the empty beats of the same Friends to Lovers arc most people I know enacted with their partners. He was a friend of a friend, we were friends for a while and got together at a music festival, he didn't go back to China, his ex-girlfriend was hurt and angry. I find it hard to be interested in that story, or inhabit the emotions I remember having, when everything that's come since the HEA is infinitely more interesting. Sometimes I feel embarrassed telling people that story, as if it could ever have any emotional weight compared to what came in the years after. A friend at work is in her sixties and has been married to her husband since she was nineteen. She said to me recently, 'Oh Flora, I'm so excited for you and Pat, there's so much good stuff in store. Something really amazing happens when you hit the thirty-years-married mark.'

As I write this, Pat is standing in the kitchen in his underwear, drinking a banana milkshake.

And yet. When I think about the party above Cuba Street or paddocks out the back of Wainuiomata, I realise that the complicated web of experience has enriched these tatty memories, that tiny kernel of our beginning. The relative flatness of our story doesn't mean that it's not also capable of being a lightning rod for complex emotions.

I haven't told Pat this, but I have a habit of listening to Shania Twain's 'You're Still the One' and thinking about him. The video opens with beach noises—seagulls, the ocean etc.—over a montage of Twain's naked back draped in shiny fabric, projected over slow-motion waves lapping onto the beach at night. She speaks breathlessly into a microphone. *When I first saw you, I saw love, and the first time you touched me, I felt love, and after all this time, you're still the one I love.* She has repeated the word 'love', in both its noun and verbal forms, three times and she's not even singing yet. It would be easy to say, *We get it, Shania.* Also: *This is very vague, Shania.* It's a cop-out to evoke a universal emotion. Way to make it meaningless. Shouldn't real art interrogate the intricacies of love, do something daring or unexpected with the concept: examine it using ironic distance, with the implication of pain, or as a construct of twenty-first-century capitalism?

But I can't help but feel, when I listen to that song, that Pat *is* still the one. Over the brushy drumming and the opening piano, Twain articulates with excruciating incisiveness some primal truth about how I feel towards him, a truth that I can't articulate myself. When I listen to 'You're Still the One' I suddenly have access to the blunt-force emotions that characterise my early experiences of love, before we really knew anything about each other. I wake up one morning and wonder why it feels like there's a helium balloon in my chest, threatening to lift me from the earth, until I realise it's because I'm going to see Pat later. Another day I am stacking the dishwasher in my flat, dazed. *What are you smiling about?* my flatmate asks, smiling at me with raised eyebrows. My lips are tender from spending a whole afternoon kissing Pat, lying together on my unmade bed.

'You're Still the One' doesn't erode the more complex emotions I feel for Pat, either. I am listening to it in my real life, after all, and I inevitably need to text him about our rates auto-payment or apologise for being so snappy before work. This is how the song becomes a vessel that can hold, for 3 minutes and 31 seconds, every single thing I know and love about Pat. I find music kind of inscrutable, so the impact of 'You're Still the One' feels like magic.

I experienced similar moments reading *Digging Deep.*
Caleb sends Drake what he and his midwifery colleagues think
is a very ugly bouquet until Drake realises that every flower,
stem and stalk is a natural remedy for Crohn's symptoms.
'Mint for diarrhoea . . . [and] turmeric. It reduces intestinal
inflammation. Same with the marigolds, or calendula as
they're also known . . . Chamomile for stress relief and
digestion, and the pièce de résistance, the peony. Its root is
used for controlling diarrhoea and cramping.' Caleb has spent
hours online researching his lover's needs.

Knowing what I know from the conference, I admire this
scene for how deftly Hogan is pulling the genre levers. She's
taken an ultra-orthodox gesture of romantic love—the Gift
of Flowers—and filled it with unexpected, original meaning.
I think she's also suggesting you can have fun negotiating
sentimentality.

And me, how do I feel reading this? I feel twenty-five. Pat
has hitchhiked back to Wellington from his mother's house
in Hawke's Bay, carrying a bouquet. He stole each flower
from a garden bed outside the Waipawa BP.

I feel twenty-nine, crying about my sore stomach after
dinner. *It's not fair,* I yelp. Pat strokes my hair. *Can I make
you a cup of peppermint tea?*

I feel thirty-two. Pat and I have just invented a game
called 'Sexy Chicken'. It goes like this: you're sitting on the
couch and you put on a love song. It's got to be a real soppy
one, like 'I Will Always Love You' or 'It's All Coming Back
to Me Now'. The longer, the better. Then you start kissing.
Touch each other. How long can you go earnestly making
out before someone laughs? A variation on Sexy Chicken is
to listen to 'Unchained Melody' and look at each other, dead
in the eyes, and see who laughs first or looks away.

*

After finishing *Digging Deep*, I learned that mm is one of the more contested sub-genres within romance fiction. Not necessarily to the general public, who are busy still wigging out about heterosexual sex, but within the romance community itself. Most romance writers and readers are straight cis women, but over the last decade mm sales have boomed and people are curious why these women might want to write and read about sex between two gay men.

Sometimes the slightly bamboozled tone this question takes seems to a) boil it down to 'but why would you be turned on by sex between two people who don't have the same genitals as you?' (easy, for a thousand different reasons) and b) miss the most obvious joy of reading anything at all—psychic mobility. But still, it's important to note that in the 2010s, as mm really started flourishing, some critics suggested mm romance was 'straight women fetishising the lives of gay men'.

And it's true that when women write mm conforming to conventional romance tropes and HEAs they can get queer lives completely wrong. *Digging Deep* ends with an epilogue in which Drake proposes to Caleb at a barbecue. Drake is down on one knee in front of all their family and friends and they're preparing for a long-term monogamous relationship together. The dominance of marriage plots and monogamy could be seen to reaffirm heteropatriarchal norms *and* appropriate queer bodies.

Similarly, Caleb is a cop, and Drake a midwife. These potentially gendered careers could code them as 'man' and 'woman', and reduce their interpersonal and sexual dynamics to heterosexual norms. But their sex roams widely and doesn't focus on anal penetration either. Reducing gay sex to this one act alone can be one of mm's biggest and most harmful blunders. Early on in *Digging Deep*, Caleb and Drake have a long, innuendo-filled discussion about how important hands and gentle touching are to sexual pleasure. In the epilogue, we also find out that Caleb and Drake are both vers—that is, men who don't have a preference for topping or bottoming in sex.

Hogan, who identified herself as queer during her keynote, wanted to talk about these dangers. 'An mm story is not an mf story with a change of pronouns,' she said, eyeballing the audience. 'Two men work completely differently than a straight couple.'

She negotiates the critiques by working closely with gay men. For *Digging Deep* she conducted a series of interviews with a friend—a gay male midwife living with Crohn's—and for every novel she uses a wide network of paid sensitivity readers. She was also keen to point out how much the tropes of mm have evolved in the last decade. Nowadays, the common mm tropes at least include 'Polyamory' and 'mmm'.[1] Reading this list aloud to the room, Hogan took off her reading glasses and shook her head. 'There used to be an awful trope called 'Out for You',' she said, 'but I consider that retrograde. Because, as we all know, ladies, no one comes out except for themselves.'

Since it was impossible to gauge the whole room's familiarity with her vocabulary, Hogan had also handed out eight pages of gender and sexuality terminology and four

---

1 Other common mm tropes: Age Gap, Bisexual Awakening, Daddy Kink, Enemies to Lovers, Fish Out of Water, Cowboy, Bodyguard, Rockstar, Shape Shifters, Geek/Jock, Drag Queen, Mpreg (male pregnancy), Sports and Small Town.

pages listing local queer romance writers. We passed the sheets around the audience.

'It doesn't say this here,' she added, 'but my romances emphasise *found family*. My characters find and create their own loving communities.'

She also explored the 'why?' question that surrounds her readers. In a Facebook fan page poll, she'd asked the 2600 members why they like to read her books, and while some answers came from gay men, answers from women included 'it's hotter than mf', 'I don't feel competition with the heroine', and 'I want to learn about other sexualities'. At this PowerPoint slide an audible *huh* went around the audience.

I really get why women are drawn to mm. I'm drawn to mm. Reading *Digging Deep* I not only relished the basic joy of reading unfamiliar sex but I also thought a lot about how long it took me to figure out my sexuality and—dare I use such a cheesy word—honour the part of me that wished to be a boy when I was little.

As an adult I am lucky that the boundaries of cis womanhood pretty much cater to my needs. I like being a woman; the word resonates with me, but the small and overtly masculine kid is still in there, kicking about in her Canberra Raiders tracksuit, wanting to be one of her brothers. Bless her, she's made it easy for me by only needing acknowledgement in quiet ways, like wearing men's clothing (usually borrowed from my husband—make of *that* what you will), and I don't often need to show people this part of me but I need to know it's still there. Although, it never hurts to be properly seen by those who love me. A few years ago Pat bought me home a Canberra Raiders league top he'd found in an op shop. He interrupted me while I was chopping potatoes and I nearly cried, getting my wet starchy hands on the heavy lime-green cotton. I've only had to claw back the teeniest sliver of wiggle room from the gender cops but I'm still shocked at how long it took me to realise that there was *any* wiggle room for me at all, and that there was a unique shape to my insides.

I feel embarrassed to admit this, but I also didn't fully understand the shape of my own sexuality until long after I was married to Pat.

'I feel like such a creep, Katie,' I said to my friend on the phone one sunny Saturday afternoon. I was standing in the supermarket alone, clutching two loaves of bread, some orange juice and a bag of peanuts with one arm. Everything threatened to tumble to the floor. I'd been wandering through the supermarket aimlessly for half an hour, retracing my steps around Newtown New World because discussing my fresh wave of queer feelings on the phone and using the self-checkout machines at the same time seemed like too much.

'Aw, that's super normal,' she said.

'Really?'

'Yes—I promise you. I've definitely felt like that when I've had crushes on, well . . . anyone who's not a cis man. I've talked to heaps of women about this.'

'Why do you reckon it happens?'

Katie paused down the end of the phone. I leaned against the freezer, looked down at the chicken nuggets.

'I dunno exactly—lots of reasons—but for one we've all definitely internalised stuff around hetero dudes being the only ones who are allowed to do the desiring.'

'Yeah, for sure . . . so I'm not a creep?'

'No,' Katie said firmly. 'It's so okay to be attracted to

people, I mean, so long as you respect their boundaries.'

I thought a lot about what she said, walking back up the hill with my peanuts and bread and orange juice. My sense of creepiness started to ebb somewhere near MacAlister Park, and in its place a teeny sun flickered to life for a moment in my chest, the centre of a miniature galaxy that was for me and me alone.

It was a total muddle figuring out I liked women. For a few months one year I was sure Pat was attracted to one of the teachers at yoga, until I realised with a thud during downward dog that it was actually me who wanted to kiss her. A year later, I finally had feelings for someone I met through weaving that were big enough to clear through the debris. Every time I looked at her I had to stop myself from saying *tell me everything you know while I kiss you all over.*

I had to ring Katie from the supermarket. Pat didn't know my weaving friend so I couldn't even pretend my feelings were his. I never told my friend about my crush on her, just did my best to quietly adore her and enjoy our friendship, though I did tell Pat on a walk one afternoon. He listened, gazing at me while we walked even though all I could do was blush and look at the ground. When I was finished, he took my hand and said that he didn't need me to be any particular kind of way, especially not super straight.

'Besides,' he said, 'I feel like our main vibe is to let each other be.'

Whatever kind of HEA that walk was, I was there for it.

For women like me, who take baby steps as we travel the landscape of our identities, or women who want to quietly enjoy the fuzziness of gender, I can see how mm is soothing and useful. The literary critic and writer Guy Mark Foster suggests that mm provides a safe place for (outwardly) straight cis women to explore the complexity of their identities. In these books they can peel their assumptions apart slowly. I thought about my first 'safe space' for challenging heterosexuality: I assumed Pat as a proxy when I wanted to sleep with my yoga teacher.

Foster cites Karen Thomas—pen name Dale Chase— who links her desire to write mm to the fact that her sexuality feels inextricably aligned with gay men and the fact that she's 'a lifelong tomboy'. 'I am a woman with a strong male side who is attracted to men,' says Thomas. Thomas identifies with both feminine and masculine ways of thinking and being, so of course her work reflects both perspectives, but it's only through her writing, through creating characters, that she gives her masculinity a *bodily* form. It's her Canberra Raiders tracksuit. Reading Foster's article, I started to think of mm books as drag shows for introverts: a celebratory performance space for playing with arbitrary and conventional sexual and gender binaries.

Foster broadly approves of Thomas's self-exploration using mm, but does raise the horrible spectre of accidentally instrumentalising other people for self-discovery. It's still very possible, even with the most sincere intentions. He also notes that the idea of 'safely exploring' inevitably evokes the converse: the relative *un*safety for cis gay men and trans men to write and publish stories that explore their own emotional and sexual experiences. It speaks to cis women's privilege that we get this space without any of the violence or oppression that accompanies it for other people.

I'm making a mental note to tell my brother that this is everything I thought about after reading a romance novel.

*

'What heat do you write?' asked my new buddy Justine after 'Sex Ed for Romance Writers', as we wandered back to the main conference room for the raffle draw and conference closing ceremony.

'I don't know,' I said, avoiding her eye. 'Actually, if I'm honest, I haven't even written a proper sex scene yet.'

Her eyes widened and she grabbed my arm. 'Oh man, me *neither*,' she said. 'We better hurry up and just get it over with, huh?' She cocked her head to one side. 'I think I'm aiming for sweet and sensuous, maybe?'

We found two seats in the main conference room and started rummaging in our conference tote bags for raffle tickets.

'Sweet and sensuous sounds so great, Justine,' I said. 'I wish I had more of an idea for my own writing.' I paused my fossicking and looked at her. 'I mean, I guess I have a sense. Like, I don't think I'll write the novel that begins *Sir Hugh woke up with a headache and a hard cock*.'[2]

'Far out, that's a killer opener, though.'

I hope that Justine has started writing her sweet and sensuous sex. I am curious about what, as Jayne Castel says, this genre will 'do' for her as it sprouts in her life. I imagine Justine carving out moments to write when her baby sleeps, or planning out scenes in her head when she drives to the supermarket on the North Shore.

The other day, clutching a stack of RWNZ worksheets, I started tentatively planning my own romance novel. The

---

2 This is the opening line of a real romance novel someone mentioned at the conference. I haven't been able to find out which, to give it the correct credit.

Heroine (H) will live with severe IBS. She will never feel sexy in the evenings because she is always extremely bloated and, though she loves fashion, she will have a difficult relationship with jeans. The Love Interest (LI) will be a [secret?] nutritionist who she meets in the waiting room at her local vet clinic. [Sub-plot: they both love kelpies.] The nutritionist will help the heroine feel sexy in the evenings in more ways than one because she will help her understand that she can manage the symptoms of her IBS, not just through diet, but with minimal caffeine, regular exercise (dog walking scenes?), and getting enough sleep. (Plot challenge cos they're having a lot of sex? How to resolve?) Two-thirds through the book the two women will realise they are each other's arch rivals in a local dog show. The HEA will see them overcome their dog-show enmity to realise they're Soul Mates. The book will be full of erotic cooking scenes where the H and LI make elaborate onion-free meals together.

And while I'm writing, if I ever think my work is silly or sentimental, I will offer myself these images from my own relationship: Pat helping me pick out onion from a restaurant meal. Pat filling a hot water bottle. Pat stroking my hair while I lie down with my head in his lap. A smile spreading across Pat's face, long-gone cigarette hanging from his lower lip, as he's illuminated by a slowly rotating party light in green, blue and red.

Author's Note

Bad Archive is a work of creative non-fiction. 'Non-fiction' because it conveys facts and describes real events, people and experiences; 'creative' because it is also a work of memory and imagination. Each real event, person and experience has inevitably been subjected to my interpretation, analyses, assumptions and projections. In some essays I have reimagined conversations from a long time ago, as well as changed names and altered timelines. In two instances I created one 'composite character' to take the place of multiple people. The truth of this book, then, is the emotional truth of my perspective. Take what you like and leave the rest.

Bibliography

On Archiving

Heming-Shadbolt, Gillian. Uncatalogued papers. Alexander Turnbull Library, Wellington.

Jenkinson, Hilary. *A Manual of Archival Administration.* London: P. Lund, 1965. Quoted in Cook, Terry. 'What Is Past Is Prologue: A History of Archival Ideas Since 1898, and the Future Paradigm Shift.' *Archivaria* 43 (February), 17–63. https://archivaria.ca/.

Mantel, Hilary. 'Why I became a historical novelist.' *Guardian.* 3 June 2017. https://www.theguardian.com/books/2017/jun/03/.

National Library of New Zealand. 'Alexander Turnbull Library Collections.' Accessed 26 October 2021. https://natlib.govt.nz/collections/.

Sheppard, F. H. W., ed. 'Norwood: Introduction.' In *Survey of London: Volume 26, Lambeth: Southern Area*, 167–173. London: London County Council, 1956. http://www.british-history.ac.uk/.

Watson, Ella Mary Marriott. Diaries, 1889, 1893–1894. MS-Papers-12038. Alexander Turnbull Library, Wellington. https://tiaki.natlib.govt.nz/.

Wikipedia. 'Upper Norwood.' Accessed 26 October 2021. https://en.wikipedia.org/wiki/Upper_Norwood.

Gather Your Strength

Billow, Alexa. 'How Seashells Are Made.' *Reactions*. 6 June 2018. YouTube video, 4:23. https://www.youtube.com/watch?v=iUeMxjkSPyM.

Proust Yourself

Birkerts, Sven. 'The Time of Our Lives.' In *The Art of Time in Memoir: Then, Again*, 3–24. Minneapolis: Graywolf Press, 2008.

Jones, Thomas and Michael Wood. 'Proust in English.' Produced by Anthony Wilks and Zoe Kilbourn. *LRB Podcast*, 11 January 2024. Podcast, 46:00. https://www.lrb.co.uk/podcasts-and-videos/.

Powles, Nina Mingya. *Tiny Moons: A Year of Eating in Shanghai.* Birmingham, UK: The Emma Press, 2021.

Wikipedia. 'Marcel Proust.' Accessed 23 October 23 2021. https://en.wikipedia.org/wiki/Marcel_Proust.

Dekmantel Selectors

Dekmantel Selectors. 'Dekmantel Selectors.' Accessed 24 October 2021. https://dekmantelselectors.com/.

DJ Mag. 'Barbarella's Discotheque.' *DJ Mag.* Last modified March 12, 2020. https://djmag.com/top-100-clubs/.

Griffiths, Sean. 'Love International.' *Mix Mag*, September 2016. ProQuest.

McDonnell, Justin. 'Interview with the organisers of The Garden Festival.' *Time Out.* Last modified 23 June 2015. https://www.timeout.com/croatia/.

Klubska Scena. 'The Garden Festival 2015. w/ Nick Colgan.' 20 July 2015. YouTube video, 1:43. https://www.youtube.com/watch?v=QbUjo_jrE4w.

Tisno Tourist Board. 'Tisno.' Accessed 26 October 2021. https://www.tz-tisno.hr/.

Julian of Norwich

Bragg, Melvyn. 'Margery Kempe and English Mysticism.' Produced by Simon Tillotson. *In Our Time*, 2 June 2016. Podcast, 45:00. https://www.bbc.co.uk/.

Jones, E. A., trans. 'Rite for the enclosing of an anchorite.' In *Hermits and Anchorites in England, 1200–1550*, 36–39. Manchester: Manchester University Press, 2019.

Julian of Norwich. *Revelations of Divine Love*. Translated by Elizabeth Spearing. London: Penguin Classics, 1998.

My Mother's Daughters

Batchen, Geoffrey. Introduction to *The Hidden Mother* by Geoffrey Batchen and Massimiliano Gioni, 4–6. London: Mack Books, 2013.

Feltham, Victoria. 'Charlotte.' In *The New Zealand Pregnancy Book*, edited by Sue Pullon and Cheryl Benn, 386–388. Wellington: Bridget Williams Books, 2008.

The Raw Material

Albers, Anni. *On Weaving*. Princeton, NJ: Princeton University Press, 2017.

Jackson, Constance and Judith Plowman. 'Getting Ready to Weave.' In *The New Zealand Woolcraft Book*, 125–141.

Auckland: Collins New Zealand, 1980.

Johnson, Sue. *Hold Me Tight: Your Guide to the Most Successful Approach to Building Loving Relationships.* London: Piatkus, 2008.

Paasche, Marit. 'Picasso and Philomena's Tongue.' In *Hannah Ryggen: Threads of Defiance.* Translated by Katia Stieglitz, 174–194. Chicago: University of Chicago Press, 2019.

Wyrm Farm

NatureHealth.com.au. 'Caring for your worm farm – worm castings and worm tea.' 25 November 2016. YouTube Video, 11:10. https://www.youtube.com/watch?v=ZAR056WD9qU&t=179s.

Megraw, Jeremy. 'The Importance of Earthworms: Darwin's Last Manuscript.' New York Public Library. 19 April 2012. https://www.nypl.org/blog/.

Tapestry Lessons

Albers, Anni. 'Tapestry.' In *On Weaving*, 48–53. Princeton, NJ: Princeton University Press, 2017.

Armour, Patricia. 'Profile.' Patricia Armour, personal website. Accessed 23 October 2021. https://www.tapestryartist.co.nz/profile.

Jackson, Constance and Judith Plowman. 'Weaving.' In *The New Zealand Woolcraft Book*, 107–120. Auckland: Collins New Zealand, 1980.

Stupples, Peter. 'Gordon Crook: tapestries.' *Tuhinga: Records of the Museum of New Zealand Te Papa Tongarewa* 31 (2020), 70–90.

Wayland-Barber, Elizabeth. *Women's Work: First 2,000 Years*. New York: W.W. Norton & Company, 1994.

Bogans of the Sky

'Dead Seagull Deterrent Decoy Scare Away Gulls.' BirdFighter.com. Accessed 6 April 2022. https://www.birdfighter.com/.

Department of Conservation. 'Wildlife Act 1953.' Accessed 22 February 2024. https://www.doc.govt.nz/.

Love, Honiana. 'Taunaha Whenua – Naming the Land.' Ngā Taonga Sound and Vision website, 20 July 20 2020. Video, 37:12. https://ngataonga.org.nz/.

Riley, Murdoch. 'Gull.' In *Māori Bird Lore: An Introduction*, 87–91. Paraparaumu: Viking Sevenseas NZ Ltd, 2001.

Parkinson, Brian. 'Southern Black-backed Gull / Karoro.' In *Field Guide to New Zealand Seabirds*. Auckland: New Holland Publishers (NZ) Ltd, 2021.

Meccanoman

New Zealand Federation of Meccano Modellers. 'About NZFMM.' Accessed 23 October 2021. http://nzfmm.co.nz/.

The HEA

Benge, Alie. 'Finding Feminism with Fabio: How Romance Novels are Unlikely Testaments to Female Power.' *Pantograph Punch*. Last modified 22 January 2020. https://www.pantograph-punch.com/.

Foster, Guy Mark. 'What To Do If Your Inner Tomboy Is a Homo: Straight Women, Bisexuality, and Pleasure in M/M Gay Romance Fictions.' *Journal of Bisexuality* 15, no. 4 (2015), 509–531. https://doi.org/10.1080/15299716.2015.1092910.

Hogan, Jay. *Digging Deep*. New Zealand: Southern Lights Publishing, 2019.

Acknowledgements

Writing this book was only possible thanks to the love and support of many, many people.

Thank you to the team at Te Herenga Waka University Press for all your enthusiasm, guidance and hard work. I am especially grateful to Ashleigh Young and Jasmine Sargent. It's been such a joy to work with you both, and Jasmine, I couldn't imagine a more insightful or fun editor than you.

Thank you to my class at the International Institute for Modern Letters for being stalwart encouragers and providing so much beautiful, perceptive feedback on my earliest, wonkiest drafts. To spend a year with you in the workshop room was the most precious gift I could imagine. To read your writing was a privilege: Leah Dodd, Bronte Heron, Zoë Higgins, Jiaqiao Liu, Scarlett McAvinue-Northcott, Sylvan Spring, Maggie Sturgess, Lachlan Taylor and Dani Yourukova.

Thank you to my MA supervisor, Chris Price, for all your time, attention, listening, guidance and meticulous feedback.

I was surprised and grateful when the draft of *Bad Archive* was awarded the 2021 Letteri Family Prize for Creative

Nonfiction. Receiving this support, and such thorough, warm feedback from people I admire has kept me writing on any tricky days since. This is the kind of encouragement I hope every new writer gets.

Everyone who appears in this manuscript has been incredibly generous in their response to seeing themselves written down, especially all the archivists and weavers who had no idea they were stumbling into essays. Thank you for your blessing. Christine Brimer and Trish Armour, your work inspires me. May I, one day, have hands half as clever as yours.

To all my colleagues and friends who made the Alexander Turnbull Library such a wild ride: thank you. What a treat to find people like you—like-minded, smart and fun—at work. Special thanks to Jess, Valerie, Susanna and Laura for your support and friendship over the years, and to Vicki-Anne and Mark for your intellectual generosity and warmth. I've learned so much from you both.

To Martha, Rose, Anna, Vera, Tania and Meg. Thank you, my hunnis, for all the kind words, dinners and unwavering care. Extra extra special thanks to Rose for reading the full draft of *Bad Archive* and giving me such incredible and helpful feedback.

To my Space mums, and Jen, Roimata, Catriona, Kate, Jasmine and Elisha: thank you for being alongside me this last year, all day, every day (especially at 4am).

As always, too, thank you Deb, for your steadfast kindness, tranquillity, good humour and wisdom.

I am also lucky to have a wonderful family, not just the people I've known since birth, but also the people I get to love now thanks to some very rad unions. To my people in Te Awamutu, New Plymouth, Wellington, Dunedin and

Sydney; Christchurch, Waipukurau, Waipawa, Napier: you are the best, you ground me.

To Vicky, Richard, Henry, Rufus, Charlotte and Humphrey. Thank you for always having my back. It's hard to put into words how much I love and admire you all, how grateful I am for everything you've taught me. Shout out to Henry for reading some of these essays in early draft, too, and being so encouraging. Vicky, you are a marvel of a copy editor. Richard, thank you for ferreting out the Sylvanian house from your shed and fixing the grain-of-wheat bulbs—in 2022.

Most of all, thank you to Pat, for all of it, every single day; for your batshit brilliant mind and for those flowering grasses you planted. You work so incredibly hard for our life together and I could not have done this without you. Without you and Tess, I wouldn't have any words at all.